**Anatomy
of the
Ship**

The Escort Carrier
GAMBIER BAY

Anatomy
of the
Ship

The Escort Carrier

GAMBIER BAY

Al Ross

Naval
Institute
Press

Frontispiece: Gambier Bay was painted
initially in Measure 14 – overall ocean grey.
The single H2-1 catapult is visible as a thin,
light line running from about the middle of
the forward elevator to the flight deck
edge. (*National Archives 80-G-222456*)

© Al Ross 1993

First published in Great Britain in 1993 by
Conway Maritime Press Limited
101 Fleet Street
London EC4Y 1DE

Published and distributed in the United States
of America and Canada by the Naval Institute Press
118 Maryland Avenue,
Annapolis, Maryland 21402–5035

Library of Congress Catalog Card No.
93–85053

ISBN 1–55750-235–8

Manufactured in Great Britain

Contents

Acknowledgements

Books of this nature require extensive research, a task made much easier and far more enjoyable through the efforts of a large number of people who graciously provide assistance and encouragement. To these individuals, the author extends his heart-felt thanks. Among the many individuals helping out (in no particular order) were A D Baker III, Paul Bender, David Shadell, William T Y'Blood, Tom Walkowiak of the Floating Dry-dock, Barrett Tillman, Bob Cressman of the Naval Historical Center, Bob Lawson, long-time editor of *The Hook*, and a number of fellow warship enthusiasts who did not wish to be identified. Special thanks go to Tony Potochniak of the *Gambier Bay*/VC-10 Association and Henry Pyzdrowski of the Heritage Foundation of the USS *Gambier Bay* and VC-10, both of whom provided reams of material that would otherwise have been very difficult to acquire.

Introduction

The *Casablanca* class CVEs were developed in response to the need for large numbers of small aircraft carriers for transport and escort duties. Earlier development had included the conversion of a small number of merchant types, primarily the diesel-powered C3 cargo types. Increased demand from both USN and Royal Navy sources caused the Secretary of the Navy to approve the conversion of twenty-four C3-S-A1 hulls in December, 1941. These new escort carriers were to be steam powered and have a single screw, with dimensions similar to their diesel-powered predecessors. Ultimately, only twenty C3 conversions, designated the *Bogue* class, were actually completed from this initial authorisation. The other four ships, the *Sangamon* class, were converted from *Cimarron* class oilers. A follow-on group of twenty-four *Bogue*s, usually referred to as the *Prince William* class, was authorised the following year. All but *Prince William* were transferred to the Royal Navy.

At this point, Henry J Kaiser entered the picture. Kaiser was a dynamic man who had been involved in a variety of major projects throughout the first four decades of the twentieth century, among which were the buildings of the Boulder and Grand Coulee dams. By the beginning of World War II, he had built seven shipyards and was building merchant vessels in large numbers using prefabrication and welding techniques. Working with the naval architecture firm of Gibbs & Cox, he developed a CVE design based on a merchant hull and presented it to the Bureau of Ships (BuShips), who immediately dismissed his concept. Undaunted, he turned directly to an old friend in the White House, Franklin D Roosevelt. Shortly thereafter, on 8 June 1942, Admiral Emory S Land of the Maritime Commission and admirals Robinson and Howard of BuShips were summoned to the White House. According to a memo prepared by Admiral Howard the same day:

> His [Roosevelt's] decision announced that more aircraft escort vessels should be started immediately. Mr. H.J. Kaiser had interviewed the President on this subject and had impressed him with the merits of a plan prepared by Gibbs & Cox (supervising engineers retained by a number of shipbuilding companies) of an aircraft escort vessel suitable for quantity production and fitted with engines capable of giving the vessel a speed of around 20 knots.

The entire programme was to be under the Maritime Commission, a fact that wrankled BuShips.

> The President desired the Navy Department and the Maritime Commission to meet with Mr. Kaiser and to make immediate arrangements to undertake this program.

The meeting was held on 9 June and the contents of its discussions were described in memos from James Bates, Director of BuShips' Technical Division:

> Admiral Land explained the circumstances surrounding the project and stated that while the design was unsatisfactory to all in a general sense, it was because there had not been time enough for thorough consideration by either the navy or the Maritime Commission. He explained that the vessel would fulfill a dual purpose. It would perform the duties of a fleet auxiliary aircraft carrier and also possibly the duties of a transport for planes.

and Admiral H S Howard of BuShips:

> Admiral Land stated that the President had ordered the Maritime Commission to take advantage of an offer made by Mr. Kaiser to construct a number of merchant vessels with a flight deck and that the essence of the program was speed with simplicity as a corollary . . . He states that they wished to get all the help they could from the Navy Department in preparing the design, but that it must be kept in mind that the ships were merchant vessels and not naval aircraft carriers or even aircraft escort vessels.

As a result of these meetings, fifty ships were ordered and designated AVG (aircraft escort vessel) 55-104. The type was reclassified as ACV (auxiliary aircraft carrier) on 20 August 1942; the final designation, CVE (escort aircraft carrier), went into effect on 15 July 1943.

The Kaiser-built CVEs (Maritime Commission type S4-S2-BB3) were produced quickly, due primarily to efficient mass-production techniques. *Casablanca* (CVE 55), the first, was delivered in 241 days; *Munda* (CVE 104), the last, was delivered in only 101 days. *Gambier Bay*, the subject of this book, was delivered in 171 days.

TABLE 1: *Casablanca* class CVE construction progress

MCE hull no.	KCIV hull no.	Name of vessel	Keel laid	Days on ways	Date launched	Days launching to delivery	Dock trial date	Sea trial date	Actual delivery date	Days keel laying to delivery
1092	301	Casablanca	11– 3–42	153	4– 5–43	88	6–12–43	6–26–43	7– 2–43	241
1093	302	Liscome Bay Sunk 11–24–43	12– 9–42	131	4–19–43	110	7–18–43	7–30–43	8– 7–43	241
1094	303	Coral Sea	12–12–42	140	5– 1–43	118	8– 8–43	8–14–43	8–27–43	258
1095	304	Corregidor	11–17–42	176	5–12–43	111	8–24–43	8–30–43	8–31–43	287
1096	305	Mission Bay	12–28–42	149	5–26–43	110	9– 4–43	9–12–43	9–13–43	259
1097	306	Guadalcanal	1– 5–43	151	6– 5–43	112	9–20–43	9–24–43	9–25–43	263
1098	307	Manila Bay	1–11–43	180	7–10–43	87	9–30–43	10– 4–43	10– 5–43	267
1099	308	Natoma Bay	1–17–43	184	7–20–43	86	10– 9–43	10–13–43	10–14–43	270
1100	309	St. Lo Sunk 10–25–44	1–23–43	206	8–17–43	67	10–18–43	10–22–43	10–23–43	273
1101	310	Tripoli	2– 1–43	213	9– 2–43	59	10–27–43	10–30–43	10–31–43	272
1102	311	Wake Island	2– 6–43	221	9–15–43	53	11– 3–43	11– 6–43	11– 7–43	274
1103	312	White Plains	2–11–43	228	9–27–43	49	11–10–43	11–13–43	11–15–43	277
1104	313	Solomons	4–19–43	170	10– 6–43	46	11–16–43	11–20–43	11–21–43	216
1105	314	Kalinin Bay	4–26–43	172	10–15–43	43	11–22–43	11–26–43	11–27–43	215
1106	315	Kasaan Bay	5–11–43	166	10–24–43	41	11–28–43	12– 3–43	12– 4–43	207
1107	316	Fanshaw Bay	5–18–43	167	11– 1–43	38	12– 4–43	12– 8–43	12– 9–43	205
1108	317	Kitkun Bay	5–31–43	161	11– 8–43	37	12–10–43	12–14–43	12–15–43	198
1109	318	Tulagi	6– 7–43	161	11–15–43	36	12–16–43	12–20–43	12–21–43	197
1110	319	Gambier Bay Sunk 10–25–44	7–10–43	135	11–22–43	36	12–21–43	12–27–43	12–28–43	171
1111	320	Nehenta Bay	7–20–43	131	11–28–43	36	12–28–43	1– 2–44	1– 3–44	167
1112	321	Hoggatt Bay	8–17–43	109	12– 4–43	38	1– 5–44	1–10–44	1–11–44	147
1113	322	Kadashan Bay	9– 2–43	100	12–11–43	38	1–14–44	1–17–44	1–18–44	138
1114	323	Marcus Island	9–15–43	92	12–16–43	41	1–20–44	1–25–44	1–26–44	133
1115	324	Savo Island	9–27–43	86	12–22–43	43	1–28–44	2– 2–44	2– 3–44	129
1116	325	Ommaney Bay Sunk 1–4–45	10– 6–43	84	12–29–43	44	2– 5–44	2–10–44	2–11–44	128
1117	326	Petrof Bay	10–15–43	82	1– 5–44	44	2–12–44	2–17–44	2–18–44	126
1118	327	Rudyerd Bay	10–24–43	80	1–12–44	44	2–19–44	2–24–44	2–25–44	124
1119	328	Saginaw Bay	11– 1–43	79	1–19–44	43	2–25–44	3– 1–44	3– 2–44	122
1120	329	Sargent Bay	11– 8–43	84	1–31–44	38	3– 2–44	3– 8–44	3– 9–44	122
1121	330	Shamrock Bay	11–15–43	81	2– 4–44	40	3– 9–44	3–14–44	3–15–44	121
1122	331	Shipley Bay	11–22–43	82	2–12–44	38	3–15–44	3–20–44	3–21–44	120
1123	332	Sitkoh Bay	11–28–43	83	2–19–44	38	3–21–44	3–27–44	3–28–44	121
1124	333	Steamer Bay	12– 4–43	84	2–26–44	38	3–28–44	4– 3–44	4– 4–44	122
1125	334	Cape Esperance	12–11–43	83	3– 3–44	37	4– 4–44	4– 8–44	4– 9–44	120
1126	335	Takanis Bay	12–16–43	85	3–10–44	36	4–10–44	4–14–44	4–15–44	121
1127	336	Thetis Bay	12–22–43	85	3–16–44	36	4–15–44	4–20–44	4–21–44	121
1128	337	Makassar Strait	12–29–43	84	3–22–44	36	4–21–44	4–26–44	4–27–44	120
1129	338	Windham Bay	1– 5–44	84	3–29–44	35	4–27–44	5– 2–44	5– 3–44	119
1130	339	Makin Island	1–12–44	84	4– 5–44	34	5– 3–44	5– 8–44	5– 9–44	118
1131	340	Lunga Point	1–19–44	83	4–11–44	33	5– 9–44	5–13–44	5–14–44	116
1132	341	Bismarck Sea Sunk 2–21–45	1–31–44	77	4–17–44	33	5–15–44	5–19–44	5–20–44	110
1133	342	Salamaua	2– 4–44	78	4–22–44	34	5–19–44	5–25–44	5–26–44	112
1134	343	Hollandia	2–12–44	76	4–28–44	34	5–26–44	5–31–44	6– 1–44	110
1135	344	Kwajalein	2–19–44	75	5– 4–44	34	6– 1–44	6– 6–44	6– 7–44	109
1136	345	Admiralty Islands	2–26–44	74	5–10–44	34	6– 7–44	6–12–44	6–13–44	108
1137	346	Bougainville	3– 3–44	74	5–16–44	33	6–13–44	6–17–44	6–18–44	107
1138	347	Matanikau	3–10–44	73	5–22–44	33	6–19–44	6–23–44	6–24–44	106
1139	348	Attu	3–16–44	72	5–27–44	34	6–24–44	6–29–44	6–30–44	106
1140	349	Roi	3–22–44	72	6– 2–44	34	6–30–44	7– 5–44	7– 6–44	106
1141	350	Munda	3–29–44	71	6– 8–44	30	7– 3–44	7– 7–44	7– 8–44	101

Service history

The keel for Kaiser hull No 319 was laid on 10 July 1943 at the Kaiser shipbuilding yard at Vancouver, Washington. Her initial Navy designation was AVG-73, and she was named *Gambier Bay*, after a small bay on the southeast coast of Admiralty Island, Alaska. Prior to launching, she was twice reclassified: as ACV-73 and, on 15 July 1943, as CVE-73. On 22 November 1943, Mrs H C Zitzewitz of Oswego broke the traditional bottle over her bow and sent her down the ways. A little over a month later, on 28 December 1943, she was commissioned at Astoria, Oregon. Her first commanding officer was Captain Hugh H Goodwin.

Following her commissioning, *Gambier Bay* proceeded to San Diego for shakedown. On 7 February 1944, she sailed for Pearl Harbor with four hundred troops and then proceeded to the Marshalls, where she flew off eighty-four replacement aircraft for *Enterprise* (CV-6). Returning to Pearl Harbor, she picked up a number of damaged aircraft and ferried them back to the United States for repair. In early March, *Gambier Bay* entered drydock at San Diego, where she was repainted and had both screws replaced to correct a major vibration problem.

The yard period was over at the end of March and *Gambier Bay* engaged in carrier qualifications for Marine pilots flying F4U Corsairs. This was the first time that the 'bent wing bird' had operated from an escort carrier deck. Returning to San Diego on 3 April, she loaded her own squadron (VC-10) aboard. On 1 May, she deployed back to the Marshalls as part of TG 52.11, which was staging for the invasion of the Marianas.

Between 15 June and 31 July, *Gambier Bay*'s VC-10 provided close air support for the Marines invading Saipan and Tinian. On 17 June, her pilots shot down a large number of Japanese aircraft attempting to disrupt the landings. Only three of an estimated forty-seven Japanese aircraft made it past the combat air patrol, and two of these were shot down by *Gambier Bay*'s gunners. On 1 August, she departed for Guam, where she again provided close air support until 11 August, when she returned to the Marshalls for repairs and replenishment. On 18 August, Captain Goodwin departed, to be replaced on 19 August by Captain Walter Vieweg. From 15 to 28 September, *Gambier Bay* supported the amphibious attack on Peleliu and Angaur in the Palaus. She then proceeded by way of Hollandia, New Guinea, to Manus, the Admiralties, where she was joined by *Kitkun Bay* (CVE-71) and four destroyer escorts. After escorting transports and amphibious landing ships to Leyte Gulf for the upcoming invasion of the Philippines, she and *Kitkun Bay* joined Admiral Thomas L Sprague's TG 77.4 on 19 September. Both were assigned to TU 77.4.3, code name 'Taffy 3', which included sisters *Fanshaw Bay* (CVE-70), *St. Lo* (CVE-63), *White Plains* (CVE-66), and *Kalinin Bay* (CVE-68).

During the morning of 25 October, 'Taffy 3' ran foul of a large force of Japanese cruisers and destroyers off Samar. In a gallant battle, lasting several hours, *Gambier Bay* was sunk by gunfire, along with escorts *Hoel* (DD-533), *Johnston* (DD-557), and *Samuel B. Roberts* (DE-413). Sister CVE *St. Lo* was sunk later that morning by a kamikaze.

Details of the battle and the damage sustained by *Gambier Bay* are provided in the following excerpts from the official action report.

Captain Vieweg's Narrative[1]

I assumed command of the USS *Gambier Bay*, which is a Kaiser class CVE, on the 19th of August 1944. At that time the ship was anchored in Segond Channel, Espiritu Santo, New Hebrides Island. Shortly after assuming command the ship proceeded in company with other carriers to Tulagi where it provisioned and prepared for participation in the seizure of Palau.

The *Gambier Bay*'s part in the Palau operation was to furnish aircraft for direct air support of the troops seizing the island and this operation was conducted without any enemy air or surface attacks reaching the *Gambier Bay*. Our planes did destroy many of the ground installations and in return received some AA fire which damaged some of our planes. But, as a matter of general interest, we lost not a single plane during the entire operation either from enemy action or operationally.

On completion of this operation we joined a force under Admiral Blandy which was to seize the Atoll of Ulithi. This operation is probably well known. It was extremely uneventful in that no Jap opposition was encountered and the island was taken over without any losses whatsoever.

Upon completion of the Ulithi operation the *Gambier Bay*, with the *Kitkun Bay* and *White Plains*, proceeded towards Hollandia with a force returning troops from the Palau operation. We gave this force air protection enroute.

After arrival at Hollandia we proceeded to Manus where we commenced preparation for the Philippine operation. The *Gambier Bay* left Manus on 8 October, with Task Group 78.2 under the command of Rear Admiral Fechteler. The *Gambier Bay* was the only carrier with this force for several days and provided principally anti-submarine protection and, in addition, furnished some utility services in the form of towing planes for ships' anti-aircraft gunnery training. We also took advantage of this time to exercise our fighters at fighter direction and to give our fighters a chance to do some dive bombing for practice on a sled towed by the *Gambier Bay*.

About the 11th or 12th of October, I do not recall the exact date, we joined with the *Kitkun Bay* and with the remainder of Task Force 78 which had come from Hollandia. These two carriers, the *Kitkun Bay* and the *Gambier Bay*, under the direct command of Rear Admiral Ofstie, proceeded toward Leyte rendering anti-submarine and Combat Air Patrol protection for the task force, that is, Task Force 78.

This force was scheduled to land two divisions in the northern part of Leyte. Upon arrival in the general vicinity of our assigned operating area to the eastward of Samar on the evening of the 19th of October, we left the task force and joined a group, Task Group 77.4, under the command of Rear Admiral T.L. Sprague. Our first assignment was actually in Task Unit 77.4.3 under Rear Admiral C.A.F. Sprague.

Commencing with the morning of the 20th, which was the day the landings on Leyte were made and continuing until the 24th and even to the 25th, we were occupied in rendering direct air support to the landing operations and occupational movements of troops on the island of Leyte.

1. This narrative by Captain W V R Vieweg describes in considerable detail how *Gambier Bay* was lost in the Battle of Samar on 25 October 1944. It was recorded on 18 December 1944 in the Office of Naval Records and Library, and this is the transcript.

We provided Combat Air Patrol, anti-submarine patrol for vessels in the transport area off Leyte. In addition we provided the same services for ourselves. Our principal job, however, was to launch air strikes against enemy ground positions which we did throughout this period from the 20th to the 24th.

The period 20 to 23 October, was quite uneventful in that we received no air attacks, and life was quite peaceful aboard ship. The 24th was routine with the exception of the fact that our early morning Combat Air Patrol managed to shoot down seven enemy planes over Leyte. However during the day and into the evening there was something ominous about the reports that were coming in about the movements of enemy ships in the eastern Philippines. It was quite obvious to me from our plots of positions of enemy forces, which were obtained from radio intercepts, that something was stirring and that the Japs were assembling a considerable force of ships including battleships and cruisers. Because of this situation, although our job was not to attack ships of this category, we realized we might perhaps be called upon to divert from our primary mission of supporting the ground operations. I had a conference the evening of the 24th, involving the executive officer, the air officer, our operations officer, the squadron commander of the squadron embarked, who was Lieutenant Commander Huxtable, commanding VC Squadron Ten. We also had the air ordnance officer at this conference.

I was particularly concerned to make sure that we were ready in case we were called upon to launch a torpedo attack. Among other things I made sure that all our pilots were recently briefed in enemy ship identification and also in the technique of torpedo dropping. They had no recent training or experience in this and I was particularly anxious to make sure that they were at least as well briefed as could be and knew the latest thoughts and techniques pertaining to torpedo dropping. In addition, quite naturally, I made sure that our ordnance gang was fully prepared to load torpedoes on short notice.

At about 2:30 in the morning I was awakened by our communications watch officer who brought me a message indicating that the Battle of Surigao was taking place. Immediately upon receipt of this message and realizing that we might have to help out, I ordered all unobligated planes loaded with torpedoes.

To clear up what I mean by unobligated planes: we had a routine schedule to meet for the following day and our forenoon demands for torpedo planes were such as to leave only four of a total of 11 Avengers on board without a prospective chore assigned. The torpedo loading was commenced immediately after issue of this order. Two planes were loaded with torpedoes and two more torpedoes were placed in the fully ready condition and could have been loaded in a few more minutes.

At 0500 in the morning we launched eight fighters to take up routine station over Leyte as Combat Air Patrol for the protection of our ground troops and transports. This flight was launched by catapult in complete darkness except for the lights shown by our screening vessels. There was nothing particularly eventful about this operation worthy of note.

At about 0620, as I recall it, the sun came up. It gives you an idea of how dark it was when our planes were launched. At 0630 we had been at general quarters, of course, since about 0430 at the time we started the warming up of planes for the 0500 launch. At about 0630 the officer in tactical command, Rear Admiral C.A.F. Sprague sent a signal by TBS to the effect that commanding officers might secure from general quarters at discretion. I secured from general quarters and went to condition 3 but remained on the bridge as did the navigator who was working up his morning position.

At about 0645 things commenced to happen. We intercepted a rather frantic voice transmission from a plane we believed was in an adjacent task unit, Task Unit 77.4.2. The gist of the message was that the Jap fleet was there somewhere about 40 miles from his home station.

We didn't have to wait long to get additional information. One of our own task unit's anti-submarine patrol planes reported the presence to the northwestward, distance about 25 miles, of a Japanese fleet consisting of four battleships, eight cruisers and 13 destroyers. Almost simultaneously there reached me on the bridge a report from the radar room, and there was visible in the PPI on the bridge a force which could be nothing but enemy since we knew of no one that should be in a position 25 miles to the northwest of us. The radar plot confirmed the report from our anti-submarine patrol.

To make certain of the situation required no great amount of thought since about that time major caliber salvos commenced falling in the center of our formation. Just prior to this contact we had been on a northernly course, which as I recall it, was 040. Only a few minutes before the contact we had reversed our course and were headed in a generally southernly direction. Immediately this contact was made and identified as enemy. The officer in tactical command ordered a course change which brought us generally to the east, and was near enough to the wind to permit launching.

Without waiting for instructions I commenced launching all planes on deck since I was under immediate threat of losing everything due to a shell hit on deck and setting the planes on fire. I managed to launch all ten remaining fighters on deck and in addition, the seven torpedo planes that were on deck. Unfortunately the torpedo planes were not fully loaded with bombs or torpedoes due to the situation.

You see we had our planes loaded for missions involving direct support of shore troops and the loading for that was a combination of some planes with 100 pound bombs and others with 500 pound general purpose bombs. Our next scheduled flight, scheduled for 1000, was an anti-submarine patrol and we were caught in the process of shifting bombs and hence some of our planes had the depth bombs in them that they would be used at 10 o'clock, some of them had nothing in them and others still had the general purpose bombs in them. Our planes, however, did much good in the air as you will find out later. They probably did delay utter catastrophy to the whole task unit.

As soon as I had completed launching the planes on deck, I started bringing up the planes from below which were the four torpedo planes which were not obligated for morning strike missions. Other planes that were brought up from the hangar deck were gassed since it was routine doctrine to keep all planes below the flight deck debombed and degassed for the safety of the ship.

By this time the officer in tactical command had changed course in small increments towards the south and when my planes were brought up on deck we had very little relative wind movement over the deck. According to the tables we didn't have enough wind to launch a fully loaded and fully fueled torpedo plane. The first torpedo plane to be launched with a torpedo in it was accordingly launched with only 35 gallons of gasoline in it. This plane subsequently launched a torpedo successfully against the enemy and then, of course, was lost.

The first torpedo plane, notwithstanding the fact that it didn't have enough wind over the deck, went off all right and I permitted the full loading of the second one with gasoline. This was launched with a full gasoline load and torpedo in it and also took part in making an attack on the enemy.

The remaining two planes were gassed fully. One of them was brought up on deck and later on jettisoned. We had changed course a little more to the south which brought the wind almost directly astern of us and there was only a five knot relative wind over the deck and I know that was certain death for the crew to catapult it and hence I pulled the crew out of the plane and catapulted the plane without a crew just as a means of jettisoning it since we were by that time threatened with hits. Salvos were falling pretty close.

During this period from about 0710 to about 0730 the enemy main body was pretty well concentrated astern of us generally to the north of us. Our destroyers made an attack at this time. All of our ships made smoke. Our planes in the air made attacks, repeated attacks, many of them without bombs. About this time a rain squall intervened and the result of all these things in combination was such as to bring about a lull in the firing from the enemy force. And also a change in their relative position.

When we came out of this rain squall at about 0830 as near as I can tell the situation was essentially this: We were still in a good formation, that is, the carriers were. As a matter of interest, there were six carriers in the formation, all equally spaced on a circle 5,000 yards in diameter. The ships were stationed in the following order, clockwise, the *St. Lo* was due north of the center of the circle. Other ships were in clockwise rotation separated by 60 degrees in the following order, *Kalinin Bay, Gambier Bay, Kitkun Bay, White Plains,* and *Fanshaw Bay.* The latter ship contained the O.T.C. and at that time was the guide.

All our destroyers, all our screen consisting of three 2,100 ton destroyers and four DEs had already left their screening station which had been a circle outside of this inner circle of CVEs. They had left and made their attack so that at about this time as we came out of the rain squall, carriers were still in this circular formation. Our destroyers and destroyer-escorts were gone away from the formation; engaged in smoke-laying operations, torpedo attacks, and gun fire.

The enemy's main body, that is, the battleships, were essentially about ten miles to the north of us. A division of cruisers of either three or four in number, probably of the *Tone* class, had gained station about 15 or 16,000 yards to the northeast of the formation. The wind was generally from the northeast. As a result the *Gambier Bay* and the *Kalinin Bay* were on the exposed windward flank of the formation where our own smoke provided very little coverage between us and these cruisers to the northeast. It did offer more protection to the other ships of the formation. And the destroyer smoke and their attacks momentarily, at least, suppressed the fire from the main enemy battleship body to the north, directly to the north of us.

These cruisers then to the northeast were in an excellent position and without opposition to pour in a rather heavy fire upon the *Gambier Bay* and the *Kitkun Bay* which they proceeded to do without delay. However, their fire was somewhat inaccurate, not very fast, salvos were about a minute or a minute and a half apart and they did not fire a particularly

large salvo, they fired four gun salvos. Apparently the *Tone* class were firing alternately the first two turrets and then the second two turrets rather than firing an eight-gun salvo. Why that was, I don't know. The pattern of this four-gun salvo was rather small. Their spotting was rather methodical and enabled us to dodge salvos.

I maneuvered the ship alternately from one side of the base course to another as I saw that a salvo was about due to hit. One could observe that the salvos would hit some distance away and gradually creep up closer and from the spacing on the water could tell that the next one would be on if we did nothing. We would invariably turn into the direction from which the salvos were creeping and sure enough the next salvo would land right in the water where we would have been, if we hadn't turned. The next few salvos would creep across to the other side and gradually creep back and would repeat the operation. This process lasted for, believe it or not, a half hour during which the enemy was closing constantly.

When the range was finally reduced to about 10,000 yards, we weren't quite so lucky and we took a hit through the flight deck, followed almost immediately by a most unfortunate piece of damage which I believe was caused by a salvo which fell just short of the port side of the ship and the shell probably exploded very near the plates outside of the forward engine room. We had a hole in our port engine room as a result of this hit or near miss which permitted rapid flooding of the engine room and made it necessary to secure. With the loss of this one engine my speed was dropped from full speed of 19½ knots to about 11 knots. Of course, I dropped astern of the formation quite rapidly and the range closed at an alarming speed.

The Japs really poured it in then and we were being hit with practically every salvo, at least one shot in each salvo did damage to the ship, although there were still occasional wild salvos. During the period from this first hit, which was around 0810 in the morning, until we sank, which was about 0910 in the morning, we were being hit probably every other minute. The hits that went through the upper structure did very little damage since the shells did not explode inside the ship. However, those shells which hit either just short or below the water line did explode and the result was that in very short order I had a flooded after engine room I had to secure which left the ship helpless in the water and without any power to provide water pressure.

Up to this time we had managed to keep our fires, started by the shell hits, suppressed, but when we lost water pressure, every hit was a small fire which soon developed into a larger one. The one remaining plane on the hanger deck was hit and caught fire, the gasoline in it caught fire. I do not think that the torpedo, torpex-loaded, exploded, but I believe the gas burned at a high rate, approaching explosion.

At about 0850 with the ship helpless in the water and with this division of cruisers passing close by and other ships of the main formation passing close by on the other side and being fired at from all sides, I ordered the ship abandoned. As we were abandoning ship the enemy ships in various directions were still firing. As a matter of fact, as the ship rolled over at about 0904, as I recall it, somewhere in there, a few minutes before she completely disappeared, there was a cruiser about 2,000 yards away still pumping it in and also still missing.

After we sank, the enemy ships that had been firing on us went about their business and pursued the remainder of our formation and disappeared from sight. However, perhaps the most alarming thing of the whole operation, from my point of view, was the fact that very shortly after we sank I observed a large Japanese ship dead in the water about three miles to the eastward. We were pretty low in the water hanging on to a life raft bouncing up and down and not feeling too well. I'm not so positive of the identification as to say that I'm entirely right. I believe it was a battleship of either the *Kongo* or *Fuso* class since the pagoda type structure would indicate such was the case. Personally, I did not see the stacks but an officer trained in identification is quite certain in his own mind that it was a *Kongo* class battleship since it had two stacks.

At any rate this ship remained dead in the water until about sunset at which time it gradually picked up steerage way to change course to the north and disappeared from sight. This ship was at all times attended by a destroyer, a two stack destroyer, which during the early stages would seem to disappear and reappear and we couldn't quite figure out what it was doing, whether it was picking up people or what. Once the ship got underway just before sunset, this destroyer continued to circle the apparently damaged battleship.

The following day, the 26th, thank God, there was no enemy ship in sight. It is a matter of conjecture with me what happened to it. We were not picked up as you can gather on the following day, in fact, towards night fall we could see the beach which we believed was Samar. We expected to be set that way by the wind and currents. Midnight the 27th passed by without our being picked up and shortly thereafter we sighted ships which we hoped were friendly. We waited until we were entirely certain of their identity at which time I fired a Very star and received a prompt reply. Some time between midnight and daybreak in the morning the bulk of our survivors were picked up.

Personally, the small group I had with me, consisting of about 150 men gathered into a cluster of rafts, was picked up about 4:30 in the morning, thereby making our cruise in the water of about two days' duration.

To go back a little bit, may I say once I got clear of the ship and was personally safe, my first thought was to assemble all the rafts into one large group. This I proceeded to do and had collected about 150 people when I observed this battleship. At that time I thought I had better quit that process since it did attract attention and the last thing in the world we wanted to do was to be captured, so I ordered the assembly of rafts discontinued and we all just laid low quietly in the water and tried to show nothing that would flash or attract attention.

As a matter of interest as to how I personally managed to get off the ship: I remained on the bridge until everyone was off the bridge and the navigator who had the deck, and I remained up there and we saw that abandoning ship process was continuing successfully and people were getting off and at that time I directed the navigator to leave the bridge and look out for himself, which he proceeded to do by clammering down the life lines which led from the open bridge.

I myself wished to make doubly sure that everyone was clear and proceeded down through the island structure. However, by this time, apparently there was a terrific fire, probably caused by the one remaining plane on the hanger deck. Smoke and hot gasses were pouring up through the island structure and I found myself in a rather embarrassing position in that I couldn't go back up on account of the smoke which was really climbing up through that area. And about that time another salvo went through the bridge structure which urged my departure. I con-

tinued, however, down to the flight deck and when I reached there, the gasses were so hot and black that I couldn't see.

I managed to feel my way aft along the island structure hoping to reach the cat walk and perhaps get aft and below that way. However, instead of walking down the ladder into the cat walk gracefully, I fell into it, not being able to see and I couldn't make out for certain where I was. In fact, I was so confused at that moment that I thought I might have gone further aft than I had and had fallen into a stack, so hot and so black were the gasses. However, I reached up instinctively. At this time I was probably prompted solely by instincts of self-preservation and grabbed ahold of the upper edge of what I was in and pulled myself up and over and started falling and a few seconds, perhaps a fraction of a second later, I broke into clear air with water beneath me. I fell about 40 feet and hit the water with quite a smack.

I had on me at that time my helmet and my pistol which seemed to help very little since it gave me a good jab in the ribs and my helmet, being secured at the time, almost choked me as I hit the water. However, I came up quite rapidly and the cold water seemed to revive me very quickly and I felt in perfectly good health except for my somewhat crippled right side which prevented my using my right arm very much.

However, I think under these circumstances the instinct of self-preservation will take care of some rather astounding damage and I had no trouble in making my way clear of the ship once I started thinking and realized I had to swim aft instead of away from the ship. I had gone over the starboard side and the ship was drifting rapidly to starboard and being set down upon me and I couldn't swim away from it at all but swam aft.

About the time I got aft to the ship, aft to the starboard quarter, another salvo went through the ship and at that time the ship was almost ready to roll over. The port side was in the water to the extent where the hanger deck was under water. I got about 100 yards off the port quarter at which time the ship very slowly rolled over to port and very slowly sank, and there was no serious detonation.

I did take the precaution to get my rear end out of the water by putting a board under it and lying on my back but apparently that was unnecessary since there was no major explosion. I've told you what I did from there on in after the ship sank. I tried to assemble life rafts until I thought it imprudent on account of the nearness of enemy vessels.

In all this account I hope you will recall that all records were lost and that I am stating things purely from memory. Times may be slightly in error, but I don't think seriously so.

As a matter of overall interest in the battle, may I say that I entered this battle with absolutely no knowledge of the fact that the enemy we encountered had come through San Bernardino Strait the night before. Information to this effect, if obtained by higher authority, had not been transmitted to this ship. I think that's about all I have to say.

Excerpts from the Official Action Report

Preliminaries

1. This ship sortied from Seeadler Harbor, Manus, Admiralty Islands, on 12 October 1944 in compliance with orders from C.T.U. 77.4.34 (Com-CarDiv-26, Rear Admiral R.A. Ofstie in *Kitkun Bay*) and enroute to Leyte Gulf it provided air cover for Groups of Task Force 78. Upon arrival in the vicinity of Leyte Gulf and at approximately sunset of 19 October 1944, it was detached and under the orders of and in company with C.T.U. 77.4.34 proceeded to its operating area where designation was changed to T.U. 77.4.32 and rendezvous was effected on 20 October 1944 with T.U. 77.4.31 to form T.U. 77.4.3. During the next succeeding five days the ship while in company with this Task Unit steamed in its day operating and night retirement areas to the east of Samar. The ship's aircraft during this period provided direct support for operations ashore and anti-submarine and combat air patrols.

2. This Task Unit's primary mission was to provide direct air support for the landing operations of the First Cavalry Division and the 24th Infantry Division on northern Leyte. In addition, the Task Unit was made responsible for:

(a) Providing Combat Air Patrol for the northern transport and objective areas.

(b) Providing a part of the Anti-Submarine Patrol for the transport area.

(c) Providing own Combat Air and Anti-Submarine patrols for the local defense of own ships against submarine and air attack.

3. Responsibility for the interception of any major surface attacks upon any units of the Seventh Fleet engaged in the support of the landings was understood to be assigned to the Third Fleet. However, this Task Unit had been enjoined 'to be ready to load torpedoes on short notice' and to be prepared to attack enemy surface forces if directed.

4. Prescribed bomb allowance for each CVE for this operation included only a limited number of 500# SAP bombs as well as the normal allowance of nine (9) aircraft torpedoes. No A.P. bombs were included in the allowance. (Note: A.P. bombs carried originally were placed ashore to make room for the increased number of G.P.'s prescribed as bomb allowance for this operation.) Thus, by inference, operations by this Task Unit against enemy surface craft were expected to be of limited scope and to be confined to those executed pursuant to specific timely directives, in each case, from authority higher than the Task Unit or Task Group Commander. No search responsibilities had been assigned this Task Unit.

5. The presence of enemy surface units to the south (Surigao Strait) was known by reason of intercepted dispatches but no knowledge existed in the ship of any enemy force having sortied through San Bernardino Strait. First knowledge of such a force came at 0645 when this Task Unit made direct contact.

6. At 0500, 25 October 1944, the scheduled objective combat air patrol of 8 VF was launched by catapult. The Task Unit was then approximately 70 miles northeast of Suluan Island on a launching course of 040°(T). This course was maintained until launchings of the other carriers had been completed and at about 0550 the course of the Task Unit was changed to 350°(T).

7. When contact with this northern enemy surface force was

established T.U. 77.4.3 consisted of 6 CVEs (*Fanshaw Bay*, Rear Admiral C.A.F. Sprague, O.T.C., *St. Lo*, *White Plains*, *Kalinin Bay*, *Kitkun Bay* and *Gambier Bay*) with a screen of 3 DDs and 4 DEs consisting of: *Hoel* (F) (DD-533), *Johnston* (DD-557), *Heerman*, DD-532, *Samuel J. Roberts* (DE-413), *Dennis* (DE-405), *Butler* (DE-339), *Raymond* (DE-341). Initially the screen was equally spaced around the six carriers which were in formation 5-R. The *Fanshaw Bay* was guide in station 2.5300. The *Gambier Bay* occupied station 2.5120 which placed her 5,000 yards bearing 120°(T) from the Guide. Insofar as the carriers were concerned the circular disposition was maintained throughout the action and this vessel held its approximate station until it was forced to drop astern by reason of the loss of one engine.

8. The Task Unit was deployed in this disposition at the time that the enemy forces were encountered. The latter's composition can only be estimated but it is generally believed by those that had an opportunity to observe it that it consisted of three or four battleships, six or eight heavy and/or light cruisers and probably at least four destroyers. In addition to this force a brief visual contact was made with a force of three destroyers to the south who responded correctly to a flashing light challenge but who did not join or take any part in the subsequent action.

Enemy ship identification

1. The following is a list of ships which came near enough (between 0800 and 0900) from the northeast and east sectors to possibly be identified by type and class: 1 *Tone* CA, 1 single stack DD, 1 *Atago* CA, 1 *Aoba* (or *Mogami*) CA, 1 two stack DD, and 1 *Kongo* BB.

2. The column of ships, 6½ miles to the NE (0745–0800) fired on by the 5" gun, was led, on a southerly course, by a *Tone* CA. The identity of the other two ships was doubtful at the time. (Note: The battery officer reported only 3 ships in column yet the SG radar operator reported and the PPI indicated 4 ships in column.)

3. The Recognition Officer, whose battle station was on the open bridge, sketched the ships at 0835 as in a loose column, (south to north) but not all in the same formation, in the order given in paragraph (1) above.

4. Two VC-10 pilots who abandoned ship from the port side of the forecastle are positive that a *Kongo* BB crossed the bow, close aboard, from port to starboard (0855–0905). As he abandoned ship the Navigator identified a *Mogami* class CA on an opposite parallel course firing from approximately 2,000 yards on our starboard beam. (Note: It is quite possible that more than 1 enemy heavy ship crossed our bow and the last would have been a *Kongo* BB reported previously as the last in the column of enemy ships.)

5. During the remainder of the day survivors reported having seen 1–2 DDs tending a BB evidently dead in the water. Also other groups reported a CA with 1–2 DDs standing by. In the first case the pagoda superstructure was the identifying feature but to some observers the width of the beam did not seem great enough to be that of a BB. In the second case the size of the ship with the absence of the pagoda superstructure identified it as a CA and not a BB.

6. Toward dark the BB was seen to swing around and hold a northerly course with at least 1 DD nearby. The speed could not be estimated but the fact that it held the same course was evidence of being underway.

7. About 0300 definite underwater explosions were felt and shortly

afterwards a large cloud of smoke was visible to a least two groups of rafts – This may have been indication of the scuttling of either the CA or BB.

8. On the morning of the 26th and thereafter no enemy ships were sighted by the survivors.

General narrative

1. At approximately 0645, 25 October 1944, Task Unit 77.4.3 made almost simultaneous contacts, through an ASP plane and SG radar, with an enemy surface force, about twenty-five miles to the northwest. This Japanese force consisted of battleships, cruisers and destroyers, estimated speed 26–30 knots, course 120°(T). Our own Task Unit was then in approximately Latitude 11–46 N. Longitude 126–09 E.

2. The six CVEs of the Task Unit were in a circular disposition within a circular screen consisting of 3 DDs and 4 DEs. Wind about 10 knots from E.N.E. Flying conditions average with numerous squalls and heavy rain showers in close proximity. Aircraft on board: 10 FM-2, and 11 TBM-1C. (8 VF had been launched at 0500 as an objective CAP).

3. Immediately the contact was identified as enemy, the OTC changed the disposition's course toward the east to a heading which was sufficiently close to the wind to permit launching and which at the same time did not tend to further close the range. Maximum speed was made, slightly in excess of 19 knots, and by 0710 all immediately available aircraft (10 VF and 8 VT) had been launched.

4. Ranges closed rapidly. *White Plains* and *Fanshaw Bay* were first taken under fire and large caliber shells were falling well within the formation with several salvos straddling those two ships. At this time, all ships were ordered to make smoke and the screening vessels left the disposition to launch a torpedo attack. Fire was opened with the ship's one 5in/38 caliber gun and observers in the ship reported that three hits were scored on the closing heavy cruisers.

5. By 0750, the disposition had been maneuvered in successive steps to a southwesterly course which left *Kalinin Bay* and *Gambier Bay* on the exposed windward flank of the formation where smoke afforded little or no protection. (Our smoke drifted to starboard and aft.) Meanwhile, a part of the enemy force had turned our flank and was closing the range from northeast. Three enemy CAs were thus in a position to close at will, since no screen remained to intervene. They maintained a heavy and disastrous fire with 8in guns while, at the same time, salvos from the enemy's main body astern fell dangerously close to the ship's side and may have caused some underwater damage not immediately apparent. Notwithstanding this concentrated fire, the ship by maneuvering on each side of the base course successfully avoided salvo after salvo until first hit at 0810. Thereafter, the ship was hit almost continuously in the flight deck and in spaces above the waterline. Few of these hangar and flight deck hits reached any vital parts of the ship. They did kill and wound a number of officers and men. Fires caused by the hits prior to loss of all power were brought under control.

6. At about 0820 the forward engine room received a hit below the waterline and with all available pumps in use flooding could not be controlled. The water rose above the level of the burners and it became necessary to secure and abandon the forward engine room at 0827. The ship slowed to 11 knots and dropped astern of the disposition.

7. Ten minutes later steering control forward was lost as a result of a hit near the island structure which probably severed liquid lines to the steering telemotor, and a subsequent hit which opened circuit breakers on the main distribution panel prevented the reestablishment of steering control at either Battle II or the trick wheel prior to the time that all power in the ship was lost. Within three minutes of this event a shell entered No. 3 boiler in the after engine room, and all steam pressure was lost. At 0845 the ship was dead in the water, there was no power and water was rising rapidly in all spaces below the second deck which resulted in a decided list to port. By 0850, three enemy cruisers had closed and were firing into the ship at point blank ranges. At this time many fires were burning within the ship, which was now listing badly to port, and it was ordered abandoned by the Captain. Approximately 750 men left the ship, taking with them many seriously wounded of whom a number were subsequently rescued. At 0907 the ship capsized to port and sank at 0911 in Latitude 11–31 N., Longitude 126–12 E. As the ship capsized, an enemy cruiser was still firing into her at a range of less than 2,000 yards.

8. Forty-five hours later, the majority of the survivors were rescued from the sea by a number of LCIs and PCs despatched from Leyte Gulf.

'Play by Play' narrative

October 25, 1944

0415 Manned all Flight Quarter Stations.

0430 Manned all General Quarter Stations.

0457 Commenced launching VF by Catapult.

0505 Completed launching 8 VF.

0616 Sunrise.

0635 Received TBS message from OTC 'Set Condition 3 at discretion of Commanding Officer'.

0637 Secured from General Quarters. Set Condition 3. Captain and Navigator on the bridge.

0640 Anti-Aircraft fire observed to the Northwest.

0643 Intercepted an almost unintelligible excited VHF transmission from an ASP plane from T.U. 77.4.2 to its base to the effect that the Japanese Fleet was sighted 30 miles from base. (T.U. 77.4.2 was operating 10 miles south of our position at the time.)

0643 A local ASP plane reported an enemy force consisting of 4 BBs, 8 CAs and/or CLs and 4 DDs.

0645 A large unidentified surface force indication appeared on SG radar bearing 300° (T) distance 23½ miles.

0645 Sounded General Quarters.

0646 OTC gave signal by TBS 'execute upon receipt 9 turn' (making new course 130°) and 'Speed 16'. Executed signal except, on orders from the Captain, engine room was directed to make maximum speed.

0647 OTC signaled by TBS 'Make maximum speed possible'.

0647 All General Quarters stations were manned.

0648 The OTC commenced passing information concerning the contacts and made urgent requests for immediate assistance to C.T.G. 77.4 and Commander Support Aircraft Central Philippines. These transmissions were in voice on 2096 kilocycles Inter-Commander Support Aircraft circuit. This circuit was loaded with this type of traffic throughout the engagement. Enemy 'Chatter' was heard intermittently on this circuit but apparently no attempt was made to effectively jam it.

0650 OTC gave signal over TBS '090 Turn.'

0652 Order given to jettison three (3) remaining napalm bombs located on No. 5 sponson.

0654 Gun flashes observed on horizon to the Northwest and large caliber salvo splashes were seen falling near the ships on the northern side of the formation. (Enemy's initial firing range estimated as approximately 35,000 yards.)

0655 All planes on the flight deck (7 TBM-1C and 10 FM-2) turning up ready for launching.

0657 Commenced launching planes.

0705 Completed launching all planes on flight deck. (This left 4 TBM-1C aboard – all on hangar deck.)

0708 Brought 1 TBM-1C up the forward elevator.

0709 OTC signalled by TBS 'All carriers launch all aircraft.'

0710 Launched 1 TBM (loaded with 1 torpedo). Destroyer screen deployed making smoke to cover the CVE group.

0715–0730 Foul weather between own Task Unit and closing enemy force momentarily checked fire and only a few salvo splashes were observed in the formation during this period.

0723 Changed course on TBS signal to the south.

0730 Picked up on SG radar two or three vessels bearing 170°(T) distance 19 miles.

0730 Enemy force, at least six separate tracks on DRT, making approaches from 270° around to about 060°.

0731 Advance cruiser unit moving around our northeast flank. Estimated speed of this unit – 30 knots. Weather partially cleared between own and parts of enemy force.

0731 Salvos splashing intermittently near *Gambier Bay, White Plains* and *Fanshaw Bay* under concentrated fire.

0732 Destroyer screen ordered by OTC to deliver a torpedo attack.

0733 One TBM-1C loaded with a torpedo brought up from hangar deck on forward elevator.

0734 Commenced pumping aviation gasoline to gas the plane now on the flight deck.

0738 Completed gassing and purged the gasoline system. (Pumped inert gas in risers to all filling stations.)

0740 OTC gave TBS order to 'open fire with the ''pea shooters'' when range is clear'.

0741 Commenced firing 5in gun at enemy cruiser 17,000 yards on port quarter.

0745 Launched one TBM, enemy salvos straddling the ship.

0745–0810 Salvos fell near the ship shortly after fire was opened with the 5in gun. During this period the ship was maneuvered to avoid salvos.

0746 Changed course to 210°(T) (on this course there was not enough wind across the deck to catapult a loaded TBM).

0750 Jettisoned one TBM by catapult. (This left only 1 plane – a TBM-1C aboard which was on the hangar deck near the forward elevator.)

0750 Three unidentified ships sighted on horizon dead ahead of formation. Sent effective major war vessel challenge on 24in searchlight. All three ships responded immediately with correct reply. On the strength of this identification (too far away to be identified by sight), on order from the Captain, the Signal Officer sent 'BT WE ARE UNDER ATTACK BT K'. The center vessel 'dashed' for each word and 'rogered' for the message.

0800 Changed course on TBS signal to 200°(T).

0805 Changed course on TBS signal to 240°(T).

0810 First hit, after end of flight deck starboard side near Batt II. Fires started on flight and hangar deck – personnel casualties small.

0815 Changed course on TBS signal to 205°(T).

0820 Hit in forward (port) engine room below waterline.

0821 Two portable electric submersible pumps placed in operation. Bilge pumps turned on.

0825 The Captain informed OTC by TBS that ship had been hit hard and had lost one engine.

0825 Engine room flooded to burner level. Boilers secured.

0826 All loads shifted to after generators and engine room.

0827 Forward engine room secured. Slowed to 11 knots, dropping astern and out of formation.

0837 Lost steering control forward probably as result of ruptured liquid lines by shell fragments from hits in or near the island structure.

0840 Radars went out of commission.

0840 After engine room hit – 8in shell entered skin of ship pierced No. 3 boiler and probably lodged in the lower part of generating tubes.

0842 Water poured rapidly into after engine room from the sea. Bilge pump suction taken in after engine room.

0843 All boilers secured on order of the Engineering Officer.

0845 Ship dead in the water. Ordered all classified material jettisoned.

0850 Gave order to 'abandon ship.' (The ship was in a sinking condition surrounded by three enemy cruisers firing at point blank range.)

0855 The Navigator, who, as Officer of the Deck, had remained with the Captain on the open bridge until then, was directed to abandon ship and did so via the starboard bridge life lines just as another salvo pierced the island structure.

0858 The Captain attempted to reach the interior of the ship via interior island structure ladders but was driven onto the flight deck then aft over the starboard side by hot black toxic smoke.

0907 Ship capsized to port.

0911 Last sign of ship disappeared from surface of the water.

0930–1230 During this period the majority of the survivors assembled into seven or eight separate groups. They lashed life rafts and floater nets together and collected sections of flight deck planking and any other floating debris with sufficient positive buoyancy to support those for whom there was no room on or around the rafts.

At least three attacks before noon by groups of four to six TBMs each with escorting FMs were observed on enemy ships to the Northeast, East, and Southeast. Inaccurate bursts of anti-aircraft fire were seen as these attacks were being made. With the exception of a large vessel with a destroyer standing by to the southeast, none of the enemy ships were seen by the survivors in the water. This particular ship has been definitely called a *Kongo* battleship by a few and not so positively identified as a heavy cruiser by others. (See Part I – Ship Identification).

1300 Dive bombing attack (6–8 SBDs or SB2Cs) to the northeast. Planes and AA bursts seen. No bomb explosions or ships observed.

1530 A group of 40 planes (SB2Cs and F6Fs) approached at 10–12,000 feet altitude from the northeast, made a complete circle around to the south, and took departure to the northwest. (Presumably in pursuit of the retiring Japanese force). As this flight circled around our group intermittent but effective bursts of AA fire were observed apparently from the ship or ship's damaged and dead in the water and by their escorts.

1800 Large enemy vessel (*Kongo* Class BB) with a destroyer nearby in sight during the forenoon still visible and observed on a northerly heading at slow speed, by some of the survivors. (Note: This ship was not seen the next morning.)

October 26, 1944

0900 1 TBM and 1 FM, together, passed five (5) miles to the east at altitude 6,000 feet. Red and green Very stars were fired and dye markers thrown in the water. The planes apparently saw none of these and continued on their northerly course.

0945 Same two planes observed at 0900 returning five (5) miles to the west on a southerly course. All attempts to attract attention were to no avail.

From time to time several groups of survivors sighted each other and closed within hailing distance.

1200 All groups were about equally spaced along either side of a line bearing 260°–080° 35–45 miles from the center of the coast line of Samar.

2230 T.G. 78.12 (2 PCs and 5 LCIs) sighted Very stars fired by various groups of survivors. (Note: This task group had been despatched from Leyte Gulf to locate and rescue the survivors of ships sunk in this engagement. They had arrived at the reported position of sinking, which was about 15 miles southeast of the estimated actual position, at 0800 26 October. This group made continual sweeps north and south with the search line running east and west until they sighted the Very stars indicated above.)

27 October 1944

0000–0430 Ships of T.G. 78.12 picked up approximately 700 survivors from the *Gambier Bay* 15–20 miles east of Samar.

0700–1000 Search was continued by C.T.G. 78.12 and survivors from the *Hoel*, *Johnston*, and *Roberts* were rescued.

1000 T.G. 78.12 departed for Leyte Gulf. (Note: There were no aircraft observed by either the survivors or the rescue vessels offering any effective assistance in the rescue operations.)

Battle damage report

Own battle damage

All times listed in this report are approximate.

0652 Damage control called the after engine room on the M.C. circuit and asked them to completely fill C-402½-F and C-402¼-F with ballast. Damage control was informed that they were completely filled. According to the oil king's report at damage control these tanks affording protection for the bomb magazine were approximately 89 per cent filled.

0652 Damage control received word from the bridge to jettison napalm bombs located on No. 5 sponson. Damage control called hangar deck control to get this accomplished and was informed that they had just completed jettisoning.

0731 Shells were landing near the ship. C & R soundings were taken and repair parties checked their respective areas and all parties reported no damage.

0810 – Hit No. 1 A shell hit about six (6) feet aft of the after elevator near the center line of the flight deck, tearing up flight deck planking and creating a six (6) foot to eight (8) foot jagged hole. The shell continued on to the after athwartship passage, then exploded in or near this passage. This caused fires on the flight deck and in the passageway. Hangar deck personnel observed smoke and flame appearing through the after bulkhead of the elevator well at the level of the gallery deck. (Note: This after bulkhead is also the forward bulkhead of the after athwartship passage.)

The after group of clipping rooms were sprinkled by Repair One. Repair One fought the fire on the flight deck and passageway, assisted on the flight deck fire by hoses manned by a unit of Repair III on the fan tail. The sprinkling system for the after part of the hangar deck and after elevator pit were turned on at this time. All fires were out within five (5) minutes. An electrical panel located in the after athwartship passsge was damaged putting the 5in ammunition hoist out of commission. The rudder angle indicator on the open bridge went out at this time probably due to a cable being cut by the explosion. A member of Repair One equipped with a R.B.A. entered the athwartship passageway to rescue personnel. This man observed a large amount of wreckage and debris but did not rescue any personnel. About 0820 word was received from the bridge to sprinkle all magazines. Damage control relayed this to the repair parties and the proper action was taken. A moment later word was received from the bridge to modify this and sprinkle only the after group of magazines. The sprinklers to the forward group were turned off. About 0834 the sprinklers to the after group of magazines were turned off.

0817 – Hit No. 2 A shell glanced off of a flight deck support on the forecastle at about frame 30 port, continued to the overhead and then down, piercing the deck and exploding in the chain locker. No fires or under water flooding were observed. There was some buckling of the forecastle deck. The fire main riser to the flight deck located near frame 30° port side was ruptured. Fire main riser valve was closed by Repair Two to prevent loss of pressure.

0820 – Hit No. 3 This shell hit the forward engine room on the port side. This was not a direct hit into the engine room itself as no fragments entered the engine room. It was an impact explosion which opened a gap in the skin of the ship approximately four (4) feet square between frames 96 and 98. The center of this hole was about twelve (12) feet below the water line of the ship. Very rapid flooding occurred in the engine room and fire room and in about five minutes the water was up to the fire box in the boilers necessitating the securing of both boilers and No. 1 main engine at 0825.

Upon receiving word of the forward engine room flooding the after engine room started No. 2 bilge pump to drain water from the forward drain wells. No. 1 bilge pump was also started. The capacity of these pumps combined is about 1,200 G.P.M. In the forward engine room the main injection to No. 1 main condenser was closed and attempts were made to open No. 1 main drain connection to the main circulator. However, due to the rush of the flooding water this was not accomplished. The concussion was sufficient to blow a foamite generator located at frame 97 against the main condenser as well as crack the 275 pound desuperheated steam line to the main circulator. This line was cracked at the first platform deck level and admitted steam into the engine room.

The engine room was abandoned shortly after 0825. The safety valves on the boiler were lifted by hand, the booster pump was secured, the fires were out of the boilers, this latter being done by closing the fuel oil quick closing valve. The main condensate and standby feed booster pumps were left running as it was difficult to secure these due to flooding. At the time of abandonment of the engine room the water was at a height of approximately five feet average. No. 2 bilge pump continued to pull a suction on the forward engine room. Two electrical submersible pumps were lowered down into the escape trunk to help control the flooding. One of the submersible pumps discharge lines was split and the pump had to be secured and a new discharge line put on.

At this time the assistant engineering officer personally evacuated the forward engine room and took station on the second deck assisting in rigging the submersible pumps. Damage control directed Repair Two and Repair Five to check the forward and after bulkheads of the engine room respectively for ruptures of the forward and after bulkheads. Repair Five reported leaks around steam lines, the port shaft and seams of the after bulkhead. This after bulkhead is the forward bulkhead of the machine shop. They were directed to use mattresses and shoring to stop these leaks and strengthen bulkheads. This work was started but not completed.

Since this hit was reported to damage control the electrical officer

shifted power from No. 1 to No. 3 generator. There was no noticeable failure in the lights at this time though there were several shorts in the circuit as the ammeter registered between 900 and 2,000 amperes. This was probably the reason for the faulty operation of the portable submersible pumps which could not maintain suction continuously.

0824 – Hit No. 4 A shell entered the skin of the ship on the port side of the machine shop at about frame 110, seven feet below the water line and exploded in the vicinity of a fresh water tank D-406-W. At this time the lights in this compartment went out and emergency lights came on. The unit from Repair Five stationed in this compartment engaged in plugging and shoring were killed or suffered serious wounds from this explosion. A unit of Repair Five that was proceeding to the machine shop for shoring was dazed by the concussion but succeeded in removing the wounded. Damage control was not notified of this hit. It was at this time that the tie breakers and the electrical panels went out and power was lost in the forward part of the ship but was soon restored.

0824 – Hit No. 5 This shell hit in compartment A-203-L on the port side nine feet above the deck at Frame 33. This shell did not explode but continued through the compartment going out the starboard side at Frame 34, four (4) feet above the deck. The only damage was a hole 10in in diameter where the shell entered and a similar hole where it went out. Fragments of steel did cut several mattresses in the compartment and a flushing system valve located at frame 33 port was demolished; however, only a small trickle of water came out as flushing had been secured. It is believed that this hit was part of the salvo which struck the machine shop. This living compartment is the main station of Repair Two.

0828 – Hit No. 6 A shell exploded on impact at frame No. 66 port side eleven (11) feet above the hangar deck. This hit gave forth smoke and momentary flame but no damage or fire was observed.

0828 – Hit No. 7 This shell hit the flight deck at frame 75, ten (10) feet from the center line (aft of the forward elevator) and started a large fire. Repair One attempted to fight this fire with hoses near the scene but there was no water pressure forward due probably to rupture of fire main risers. They then proceeded to run a jumper from the after section of the ship. By the time this was accomplished all pressure was lost on the fire main due to the hit in the after engine room.

0830 – Hit No. 8 A shell exploded in the C.P.O. galley. The inboard bulkhead of the pantry was bellied out. This dislocation of the bulkhead blocked the passageway which leads to the forward messhall for about a distance of eight (8) feet. No fires were observed. A piece of metal from this explosion severely cut the leg of a wounded man lying in the wardroom (STONE, Harold Roger, 287-51-84, Mlc, USN).

0832 – Hit No. 9 A shell hit the starboard bulkhead of the forward messhall at about frame 114 which apparently exploded on impact tearing a hole about three (3) feet by four (4) feet in size out of this bulkhead. Damage control received no report of this hit at the time it happened.

0837 – Hit No. 10 A shell hit and exploded in steward's mates compartment C-202-2L. This shell may have exploded on impact. No fires were observed from this hit. Bunks and lockers were wrecked. Lights went out and compartment was filled with smoke. (This may have caused loss of power in the steering engine room due to concussion.)

17

0837 – Hit No. 11 This shell hit and exploded on impact against the after messing compartment bulkhead port side. This caused a rupture of the bulkhead between frames 159–165. A piece of shrapnel hit the after distribution board entering on the port side knocking out the tie breakers which caused loss of power in the after section of the ship. The board was still receiving power at this time from the after engine room as the indicator lights did not fail. Port ladder in this messhall leading to the hangar deck was torn off. Five or six men were dazed. This is the main station for Repair Three and is used as an after battle dressing station.

0837 – Hit No. 12 A shell came through the port side of the after engine room about ten (10) feet below the ships normal water line at frame 124. The hole made by the shell is estimated to have had a diameter of one foot. This shell passed through the air casing around No. 3 boiler and entered the boiler. As far as it is known it pierced the generating tubes and lodged in the boiler. This hit knocked the fuel oil quick closing valve off the fuel oil line and the fuel oil supply was cut off to the burners by closing the fuel oil throttle valve. The water flooded through the hole with such force that it spouted up against the casing of No. 3 boiler. This rendered it impossible to observe the actual damage to the boiler. At this time the bilge suction of No. 2 bilge pump which was pumping from the forward engine room was shifted to the after drain well. Aside from the damage to No. 3 boiler necessitating the socuring [sic] of it, the concussion (from this shell or another of the same salvo) split the skin of the ship vertically, at frame 119 port side. This split was ten feet long by one-half ($\frac{1}{2}$) inch wide and was entirely under the water line and was also flooding at the same time that No. 3 boiler was hit. The lights went out for a few seconds indicating a power failure. This was probably due to the after distribution board being hit (see Hit No. 11), however, emergency battle lanterns operated satisfactorily.

Due to the excessive flooding with the consequent danger of explosion in No. 4 boiler this boiler and No. 2 main engine was secured. This was about 0845.

The main drain of No. 4 main circulator was opened in an attempt to check flooding but the circulator did not draw as was evidenced by the fact that upon opening the circulator suction to the bilge the turbine speeded up considerably. About seven minutes after the first hit the water was last observed rising over deck plate leaves.

0843 – Hit No. 13 A shell hit the after part of the engine room at frame 134 port side, first platform deck about where No. 4 ventilation fan is located. Damage or effects of this hit were not noted. This hit was probably below the water line at this time due to the port list of the ship. The Engineering Officer personally reported these hits to Damage Control as the phone circuits from the after engine room to this station were dead at this time. This report was then relayed to the bridge from Damage Control over the JA circuit.

As a result of the uncontrolled flooding of the forward engine room, machine shop and after engine room, the ship's G.M. was rapidly becoming negative.

0850 – Hit No. 14 A shell hit entered the port side of G.S.K. about frame 79. A large explosion was heard and felt (Note: G.S.K. is just forward of the forward engine room). The port hatch to G.S.K. at the first platform deck was blown open. The CO_2 built-in system control was broken causing the CO_2 to start flooding in G.S.K. Flooding had commenced. No action could be taken.

0850 – Hit No. 15 A shell hit a TBM which was located on the hangar deck in the vicinity of the forward elevator. This hit caused the gasoline tanks of the plane to explode which caused considerable damage to the forward part of the hangar deck and started fires on the hangar deck and in the forward elevator pit. A group from Repair Two led a hose out from the C.P.O. quarters but no pressure was on the line. A large number of men abandoning ship by way of the hangar deck were killed and wounded by this explosion. The CO_2 built-in system in the gasoline pump room, alcohol locker and acid locker was turned on at this time.

In addition to the hits described above, there were numerous other shell hits as well as many near misses. Information regarding many of these hits is very incomplete due to the fact that the observing personnel in the vicinity were either killed, wounded or dazed or engrossed in abandoning ship. These hits together with what information is known are listed below. Times of all these hits are either unknown or indefinite.

No. X-1 Conditioning Room (Gallery Deck Battle Dressing Station). Lieutenant Commander Stewart (MC) was believed killed by a hit in this compartment. Damage unknown.

No. X-2 Catapult Track. A shell landed and exploded on or about the Catapult Track on the flight deck tearing up planking and the catapult track. No fire. No damage noted.

No. X-3 A shell hit on the starboard side of the gallery between guns 41 and 43. This hit apparently exploded on impact with the outboard bulkhead of Radar Room No. 1 or exploded immediately on entering this compartment. Smoke was observed but no reports on any fires was received. This hit killed and wounded personnel on guns 41 and 43 and in radar room.

No. X-4. A shell penetrated the passageway at the port side in the area between the executive officers stateroom or just forward of the executive officers stateroom. It made a large hole in the passageway deck and quite a concussion was felt by personnel in the vicinity, some of whom were wounded by shrapnel or splinters. The path of this shell is not known but it is possible that it could have caused the wreckage later observed in the officers toilet and shower located on the upper deck. No action was taken in regard to this hit, nor report made at the time to either damage control or any repair party. Time of this hit is indefinite but personnel state that it was only shortly before abandoning ship.

No. X-5. J.O. Bunkroom on gallery deck and Captain's Cabin. A shell exploded in the vicinity of these two compartments. Have no report on damage sustained. It has been reported that two men were killed in the J.O. Bunkroom.

No. X-6. Shells hit the gallery catwalk just forward of Repair One and just aft of No. 2 stack. Only damage observed was rupturing of catwalk in this vicinity and the demolishing of one life raft.

No. X-7 A shell hit the forward port corner of the flight deck. Only damage observed was splintering of the flight deck in that vicinity.

No. X-8 Pilot House. A shell was observed entering the port side of island structure at the pilot house level. It set off a CO_2 fire extinguisher but caused no other damage. At this time steering control had already been lost which would place the time of this hit between 0837 and 0845.

No. X-9 SK Radar. A shell was also noted to hit the SK radar antenna. Only damage noted was a portion of radar grid knocked into the water.

No. X-10 A hit caused a lot of wreckage in the forward elevator machinery room. Have no report as to where this shell entered the ship. Though the time of this hit is indefinite, it is known from the statement of the electrician mate stationed in the forward elevator machinery room that this space was intact up to 0840.

No. X-11 A shell hit the clipping room forward of the communication office on the port side gallery at the time personnel were abandoning ship. Damage unknown.

While in the water after abandoning ship numerous men heard a large explosion and observed the forward elevator being blown into the water.

Gambier Bay was awarded four battle stars and shared a Presidential Unit Citation with the other ships of 'Taffy 3'.

General arrangement and hull structure

Gambier Bay's hull was typical of the mass-produced *Casablanca* class CVEs produced by Kaiser Co Inc. Of all-welded construction, the prefabricated hull incorporated flight, gallery, upper, hangar, second, and first platform decks, with only the flight, gallery and hangar decks being continuous.

Hull construction incorporated nine strakes of welded plates over longitudinal stringers and 204 transverse frames. Plating ranged from 20.4# to 30.6#, the bulk being 22.95# STS. Frame spacing varied as follows:

Frames	Spacing
0–14	2ft 0in
14–32	2ft 3in
32–185	2ft 6in
185–204	2ft 0in

The engineering spaces combined engine and boiler in the same flat, with the two flats separated by settling tanks and shops. The forward engine drove the port screw, the aft engine the starboard screw. Eighteen fuel oil tanks were provided, nine of which were below the engineering spaces. Two AVGAS tanks were located below the first platform deck between frames 50 and 64, separated from the fuel oil tanks by a cofferdam at either end. The tank top spaces provided stowage for ammunition and general stores.

Crew berthing was on both the first platform and second deck, while CPOs were berthed forward on the hangar deck. Officer staterooms were located on the first platform deck between frames 63 and 82, and on the upper deck forward.

The hangar, measuring about 256ft × 56ft with a height of 17ft 6in, was unobstructed and extended from frame 46 to frame 184. An elevator was fitted at each end of the hangar to expedite air operations and stowage, especially when the ship was in a transport mode. The ship's only 5in/38 was mounted on the extreme aft end of the hangar deck.

TABLE 2: **Ship's particulars**

Class	*Casablanca*
Length overall	512ft 3in
Length between perpendiculars	490ft 0in
Beam (waterline)	65ft 0in
(extreme)	108ft 1in
Flight deck	474ft × 80ft
Hangar deck height	17ft 6in
Draught (mean)	20ft 9in
Displacement (design)	9570 tons
(full load)	10,200 tons
Shaft horsepower (shp)	9000
Speed	20kts
Range	7200nm @ 19kts
Armament	One 5in/38 Mk30
	Four twin 40mm Mk1
	Twelve 20mm Mk4
Aircraft	Eighteen FM-2 Wildcats
	Twelve TBM-1C Avengers

Sponsons were mounted outboard on either side at the hangar deck level for refuelling and underway replenishment.

The gallery deck, located directly below the flight deck, was honeycombed with office spaces, ready-rooms, and clipping rooms for the 20mm and 40mm guns. Catwalks and shielded gun tubs were ranged along the edges of the gallery deck. Access to the gallery deck spaces was through a large number of doorways, while inclined ladders from the catwalks provided access to the flight deck.

The flight deck was prefabricated in nine sections, the front section weighing 80 tons. Expansion joints were installed at frames 47, 101, and 146. A 34ft × 42ft elevator was installed between frames 49 and 66, while a 38ft × 42ft unit was fitted aft between frames 169 and 184. The deck was planked with 3in × 6in fir, separated by fifty-eight steel aircraft tie-down strips spaced between 7ft and 9ft 6in. The number of planks between each strip varied with the spacing.

Twelve sets of arresting gear ran across the flight deck between frames 68 and 176. The forward three sets incorporated two-cable crash barriers attached to large pivoting arms let flush into the deck.

An LSO platform and safety net was placed aft on the port side of the flight deck. An H2-1 catapult was mounted on the flight deck forward, to port and parallel with the centreline of the ship.

The island was a compact, simple box structure just over 6ft wide, containing three decks and offset to starboard. The gallery deck level contained radio and chart rooms. The captain's and navigator's sea cabins were at flight deck level, and the navigating bridge level contained the steering station and another chartroom. Gunnery control was provided on the open observation platform. A large lattice mast was incorporated into the bridge structure, and served as a platform for the two 24in searchlights, SG, SK, and YE radar aerials. An RDF antenna hung below the aft portion of the observation platform. A large aircraft-handling boom was mounted on the face of the bridge at flight deck level.

Machinery

Gambier Bay was powered by two 5-cylinder reciprocating Uniflow engines developing a combined 9000shp. Steam to operate the engines was provided by four Babcock & Wilcox Express D boilers which developed 285psi at 577°F.

Steam turbines were in short supply when Kaiser was developing the *Casablanca* class CVEs. As a result, he acquired the manufacturing rights to build the Skinner Uniflow (or Unaflow) reciprocating engine. The original concept for the uniflow engine had been developed in England in 1885 by J T Todd and later refined by Professor J Stumpf in Berlin. Essentially, the Uniflow engine was an enclosed, vertical unit in which all cylinders were identical; double-beat poppet valves were used for steam intake, and steam was exhausted through a ring of ports in the centre of the cylinder wall. Control was by cut-off from levers mounted on the side of the engine. While the original versions had proved troublesome in operation, Kaiser modified his to overcome the major defects. BuShips was not enthusiastic about the use of such engines, but had little choice in the matter, as the development of these carriers was being carried out by the Maritime Commission.

Catapult

Casablanca class CVEs were fitted with a single H2-1 catapult on the port side of the flight deck. The initial charge for this catapult operated at 2500psi but was downrated to 1900psi in July of 1943 due to complaints of excessive end speeds. Maximum aircraft weight was 8800lb, which presented a major operational limitation. While a fully-loaded FM-2 weighed about 82000lb, a fully-loaded Avenger weighed over 13,000lb. A COMCARDIV 26 memo dated 10 October 1944, referring to the *Casablanca* class CVEs, observed that:

> with a sustained top speed of 18 knots, operation is absolutely marginal under no-wind conditions: the loading of VT aircraft must be cut approximately in half for safe catapulting. The FM-2 is just able to get into the air with almost a full deck free run, and both types are uncomfortable in landing.
> . . . The ships have a single catapult. Failure of this equipment means that only the FM-2 can be operated.

Radar

Gambier Bay carried the standard radar suite of the period: SG and SK, with a YE aircraft homing beacon. No fire control set was fitted.

SG

The SG, first developed by Raytheon in 1941, was a 10cm surface search radar with a range of approximately 22nm, depending upon the size of the target. In the case of large groups of ships, the range was even greater. *Gambier Bay*'s action report for 25 October 1944 notes that the Japanese task force was detected at 23.5 miles.

A relatively small unit, the SG weighed about 3000lb and incorporated a waveguide-fed 48in × 15in parabolic antenna, which was mounted on a pole mast attached to the aft end of the lattice mast. In action, the SG was also the nearest thing to fire control radar carried by the CVEs, although its use was limited to establishing initial target range.

SK

Gambier Bay's other radar was the SK, the standard large-ship air search unit. The antenna assembly consisted of a large 17ft square reflector with a 6×6 dipole array and weighing over 2300lb. The range was 100 nautical miles at 10,000ft.

Fire control equipment

Fire control for *Gambier Bay* was limited to the MK51 director fitted with the MK14 computing gunsight and, initially, a 2.5m optical rangefinder.

MK51 director/MK14 gunsight

Gambier Bay carried four MK51 directors to control the 40mm mounts at each end of the flight deck. The MK51 director was a simple lightweight director consisting of a pedestal, head, and, initially, a simple ring sight. Later, the ring sight was replaced with the MK14 computing gunsight. The pedestal was bolted to the deck and supported the head on ball bearings. The head supported a carriage which had a platform for mounting the gunsight. The handle bars attached to the carriage were used by the operator to move the carriage in elevation and the head in train. The right handle contained a firing key which controlled the guns when they were in a director-control mode. The sight power unit, which consisted of a motor-driven air pump, was mounted on the head.

The MK14 gunsight, developed by Dr Charles Draper of MIT, was mounted on both the MK51 directors and the 20mm guns. It incorporated two gyroscopically-operated mechanisms which automatically computed lead angle and super elevation. Lead angle computations were always correct for any value of trunnion tilt, and super elevation was computed and applied in the vertical plane. A luminous cross which established the sighting axis was the reflected image of an illuminated reticle. Sight movement during tracking caused the two gyroscopes to process, actuating the two mirrors which shifted the position of the cross. The offset of the cross was such that the sighting axis was displaced from the bore axis by the required lead angle corrected for super elevation.

2.5 metre rangefinder

As built, *Gambier Bay* carried a 2.5m rangefinder mounted on a platform just forward of the mast until at least February 1944. By July 1944, however, it was replaced by two sky lookouts.

Searchlights

Two 24in searchlights were initially mounted on a platform on the fore and aft sides of the lattice mast. By July 1944, only the forward searchlight remained.

Aircraft

At the time of her loss, *Gambier Bay* embarked VC-10, a typical CVE composite squadron consisting of eighteen FM-2 Wildcat fighters and twelve TBM-1C Avenger torpedo bombers.

FM-2

The FM-2 Wildcat was developed specifically for service aboard the CVEs. In 1942 the Navy issued a request for a lightweight fighter that could operate from the short flight decks of the escort carriers coming into service. In response, Grumman lightened an F4F airframe, installed the more powerful Wright R-1820-56, and deleted two of the .50 calibre Browning wing guns. This airframe, BUNO 12228, was designated the XF4F-8 and first flew in November 1942. A second airframe, BUNO 12229, had its vertical stabiliser and rudder lengthened 8.5in to counteract the increased torque of the Wright engine and became the prototype for the FM-2.

Although a Grumman design, the FM-2 was built by the Eastern Aircraft Division of General Motors. In early 1942, Grumman had contracted with GM to take over production of the F4F-4 so that the parent company could concentrate on the development of the new F6F Hellcat. GM's version of the F4F-4 was designated the FM-1 and was identical to its Grumman counterpart except that it had four instead of six wing guns. In the spring of 1943, GM began producing the FM-2 and delivered its first aeroplane to the Navy in September.

TBM-1C

Like the FM-2, the TBM-1C was a Grumman design produced by Eastern Aircraft. Essentially, the TBM-1C differed from the earlier TBM-1 primarily in armament. Pilots had complained that the cowl-mounted .30 calibre machine-gun of the TBM-1 was entirely inadequate and had even experimented with externally-mounted .50s in an effort to increase forward firepower. Based on these complaints, Grumman revised the wing structure and fitted a single .50 calibre Browning with 600 rounds in each wing, just outboard of the wing fold joint. The Avenger normally carried a single MK13 aircraft torpedo, although 500lb bombs or 350lb depth charges could be substituted.

Aircraft camouflage and markings

Both aircraft types were painted in the then-current tricolour scheme of non-specular sea blue (AN 607) upper surfaces, non-specular intermediate blue (AN 608) fuselage sides and vertical tail, and non-specular insignia white undersides. Photographic evidence, however, indicates that some of VC-10s FM-2s were painted overall gloss sea blue (AN 623). A large white block letter 'B' was applied to the vertical tail fin of all aircraft.

Armament

Gambier Bay's armament was typical of her class and designed primarily for anti-aircraft defence: one 5in/38 open mount; eight twin 40mm; and twenty single 20mm.

5in/38

A single, dual-purpose 5in/38 Mk30 open mount was fitted on the fantail. The gun was a Mk12 and comprised the barrel, housing, and breech mechanism. The barrel was a radially-expanded monobloc unit weighing about two tons and secured to the housing through a bayonet joint. The housing, about 5ft long, incorporated the mountings for the barrel, recoil cylinders, and breech mechanism. The breech mechanism was a vertical sliding wedge, semi-automatic unit.

The 5in/38 used semi-fixed ammunition consisting of a 54lb projectile and a case assembly weighing about 22lb, including a 15lb powder charge. Projectile types included anti-aircraft, common, illuminating, and smoke. Average muzzle velocity was about 2600ft per second.

During the action off Samar, *Gambier Bay*'s 5in mount first opened fire on a Japanese cruiser about 17,000yds astern. Since no fire control radar was fitted, initial range was obtained through CIC from the SG radar. Subsequent corrections had to be made visually. Shortly after commencing firing, the electrical system was knocked out and the gun had to shift to manual control. She was able to get off about thirty rounds before several near misses jammed the rammer, putting the gun out of commission. Her battery officer observed three probable hits on two cruisers, but these were determined to have had little effect. The first hit, observed at 0750, was on the No. 2 turret of the leading cruiser at a range of 14,000 yards. Two minutes later, a second shell hit the cruiser's stern, its range about 13,500 yards. The third and final hit, at 0755, struck another cruiser abaft the funnel, causing superficial damage.

TABLE 3: **Particulars of aircraft**

FM-2 Wildcat	
Wingspan	38ft 0in
Length	28ft 7 7/32in
Height (3-point position)	9ft 1 1/2in
Width (wings folded)	14ft 4in
Height (wings folded)	9ft 9in
Engine	Wright R–1820–56W
Horsepower	1300
Gross weight	8221lb
Service ceiling	35,600ft
Max speed	319kts @ 19,600ft
Armament	Four .50 calibre mgs
TBM-1C Avenger	
Wingspan	54ft 2in
Length	40ft 4 23/32in
Height (3-point position)	15ft 5 1/32in
Width (wings folded)	19ft 0in
Height (wings folded)	12ft 0in
Engine	Wright R–2600–20
Horsepower	1700
Gross weight	13,667lb
Service ceiling	21,400ft
Max speed	271kts @ 12,000ft
Armament	Three .50 calibre mgs
	One .30 calibre mg
	One Mk13 torpedo

5in/38 Mk30

Type	Dual purpose, open, base ring
Gun	Mk12 Mod 1
Max powder pressure	18 long tons per sq in
Barrel weight	3990lb
Total weight	37,700lb
Oscillating weight	13,800lb
Recoiling weight	8150lb
Max trunnion pressure	91,300lb
Muzzle velocity (feet per second)	2600
Max range	18,200 yards @ 45 degrees 10 minutes elevation
Elevation limits	−15 degrees to +85 degrees
Ammunition	Projectiles
	Common – 54lb
	AA Common – 55.2lb
	Illuminating – 54.5lb
	Cartridge
	Case – 12.3lb
	Charge – nominal 15.2lb

40mm Mk1

Type	Twin mount, open, base ring
Gun	Mk1, 40mm/60
Max powder pressure	19.5 long tons per sq in
Barrel weight	202lb
Total weight	13,200lb
Oscillating weight	2300lb
Recoiling weight	490lb per gun
Muzzle velocity (feet per second)	2890
Max range	11,000 yards @ 42 degrees elevation
Elevation limits	−15 degrees to +90 degrees
Ammunition	Projectiles
	AA (one projectile) – 1.98lb
	AA (one round) – 4.75lb
	AP (one clip) – 20lb
	Cartridge
	Case – 1.89–1.92lb
	Charge – 315 grams

20mm Mk4

Type	Single mount, manual
Barrel weight	150lb
Cyclic	450rpm
Muzzle velocity (feet per second)	2740
Max altitude	10,000ft @ 90 degrees elevation
Max range	4,800 yards @ 35 degrees elevation
Ammunition	HE
	Projectile – .0271lb
	Case – .190lb
	Charge – 27.7 grams
	ADP
	Projectile – .0268lb
	Case – .180lb
	Charge – 27.7 grams
Elevation limits	−15 degrees to +90 degrees
Shield	0.5in
Shield weight	250lb
Total weight	1540lb
Brake load	1785lb

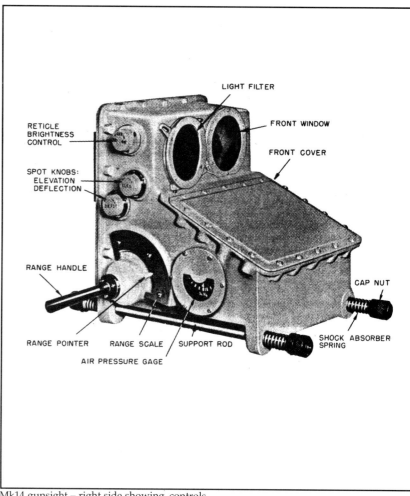

Mk14 gunsight – right side showing controls.

Long-range AA

The primary long-range anti-aircraft weapon on *Gambier Bay* was the twin 40mm Mk1, mounted in pairs on either side of the flight deck, fore and aft. These mounts were power-driven, water-cooled units having both local and automatic control, the latter being provided by the versatile Mk51 director and its associated Mk14 gunsight. Under power operation, the training rate was 30 degrees per second. Elevation limits were minus 15 degrees to plus 90 degrees, with an elevation rate of 24 degrees per second.

The weapon was a recoil-operated heavy machine-gun designed primarily for anti-aircraft fire. Its distinctive features included a liquid-cooled barrel, vertical sliding-wedge breech mechanism, hand-fed automatic loader, and spring-operated rammer. The trigger mechanism controlled the rammer operation only; once the ramming cycle started, the round was loaded and fired automatically without further control. The gun could be set for single or automatic fire, the firing rate in automatic being about 120rpm.

Short-range AA

Gambier Bay carried a total of twenty single, shielded 20mm Mk4 Oerlikon mounts in her flight deck galleries. The gun itself was a 20mm/70 calibre weapon consisting of four main groups:

- barrel and breech casing
- breechblock
- recoil and counter-recoil system
- trigger mechanism and locking device.

Designed for automatic firing only, the gun used some of the force developed by the explosion of the propellant to eject the empty cartridge, cock, reload, and fire the next round.

The 20mm fired fixed ammunition from a sixty-round magazine at a cyclic rate of about 450rpm. In practice, an experienced crew could maintain a rate of about 300rpm. Usually, every other round or every third round in the loaded magazine was a tracer.

The Mk4 mount featured a cast pedestal and a variable height trunnion bracket. The pedestal was bolted to the deck, but the pedestal head, through which the column rose, rotated about the top of the pedestal and could be locked in any position by a clamping lever. The column could be raised about 15in by a handwheel mounted on the head. Mounted on top of the column were the trunnion bracket and pivot, which also provided support for the shield, cradle spiral spring, and cradle, to which the gun was bolted. The cradle spring, mounted around the left trunnion, had one end attached to the trunnion and the other to the spring case, thus acting as a counterbalance to the weight of the gun. Adjustable shoulder rests and a ring sight were standard, as was a 0.5in thick shield weighing nearly 250lb.

Ship's boats

Two 26ft motor whaleboats were carried, slung beneath the flight deck on either side. These were the standard wooden, carvel-planked craft used on practically all USN warships of the period. Thirty twenty-five-man life rafts and eight twenty-five-man floater nets provided additional survival equipment.

Camouflage

Gambier Bay is known to have carried at least two schemes during her short life. Until February 1944 she was painted in Measure 14 – overall ocean grey (5-O). At the time of her loss, in October 1944, she was painted in Measure 32/15a – pale grey (5-P), light grey (5-L), ocean grey (5-O), and black. Exposed metal decks were painted deck blue (20-B), while the flight deck was either blue flight deck stain (No. 21) or a later, darker stain similar to deck blue. Flight deck stripes were originally white or light grey, but photos taken in mid-1944 show the stripes as either worn completely off or painted a shade similar to the flight deck. A large black '73' was carried on the forward end of the flight deck.

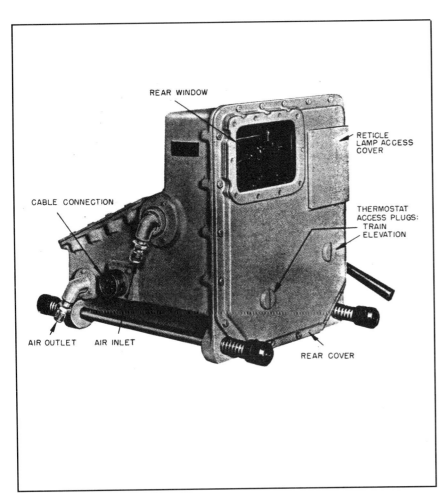

REAR WINDOW

RETICLE
LAMP ACCESS
COVER

CABLE CONNECTION

THERMOSTAT
ACCESS PLUGS:
TRAIN
ELEVATION

AIR OUTLET   AIR INLET

REAR COVER

Mk14 gunsight – left side and rear.

Notes on sources

The primary materials used to develop this book included a large number of drawings, manuals, and official documents obtained from a variety of sources such as the Naval Historical Center, National Archives, the *Gambier Bay*/VC-10 Association, and a number of private sources.

For readers wishing to learn more about *Gambier Bay*, other escort carriers, and their air groups, the following books are suggested:

Dresser, James, *Escort Carriers and their Unit Markings during WWII in the Pacific*. Published by the author 1980.

Friedman, Norman, *U.S. Carriers – An Illustrated Design History* (Annapolis 1983).

Hoyt, Edwin, *The Men of the Gambier Bay* (New York 1979).

Poolman, Kenneth, *Allied Escort Carriers of World War Two in Action* (Annapolis 1988).

Terzibaschitsch, Stefan, *Escort Carriers and Aviation Support Ships of the U.S. Navy* (New York 1981).

Tillman, Barrett, *Avenger at War* (Annapolis 1990).

Tillman, Barrett, *Wildcat* (Annapolis 1983).

Y'Blood, William T, *Hunter-Killer* (Annapolis 1983).

Y'Blood, William T, *The Little Giants* (Annapolis 1987).

The Photographs

Various stages of *Gambier Bay* under construction. In the first photograph, the tank tops are under construction; in the next, the hangar deck appears just about completed; last, the flight deck is nearly finished and the ship almost ready for launching. (*A Potochniak collection*)

The port side of *Gambier Bay*'s superstructure. Sky lookouts have replaced the 2.5m optical rangefinder and the aft 24in searchlight has been removed from its platform. (*National Archives 80-G-243853*)

Bow view of *Gambier Bay* in drydock, April 1944. (*National Archives 80-G-232200*)

The broad flat transom of the *Casablanca*s required the 5in/38 mount aft be heavily supported by girders. (*National Archives 19-N-74931*)

Port side of the Measure 32/15a carried by *Gambier Bay* at the time of her loss. Apparently, the censor has airbrushed out the SG and SK antennae, as neither are visible on the original print. (*National Archives 80-G-46892*)

The compact size of the island is apparent in this photo of *Natoma Bay* (CVE-62) taken on 16 June 1944. (*National Archives 80-G-275983*)

'Any landing you can walk away from . . .' This TBM-1C came to grief on *Kalinin Bay* (CVE-68) on 7 June 1944. Details of the uptake and the walkway over it are plainly visible. (*National Archives 80-G-235942*)

Kalinin Bay during the battle off Samar, 25 October 1944, in which *Gambier Bay* was sunk. One of the crash barrier arms and related wires can be seen in the foreground. (*National Archives 80-G-270509*)

Gambier Bay making smoke during the battle off Samar, 25 October 1944. Lt Hank Pyzdrowski's Avenger can be seen on the catapult. It was later launched, unmanned, to clear the deck. (*National Archives 80-G-288159*)

The FM-2 was designed specifically to operate from the CVEs. This particular aircraft is being moved on to the forward elevator of *Makin Island* (CVE-93). (*National Archives 80-G-301245*)

A damaged VC-10 FM-2 being jettisoned on *Gambier Bay*, 18 June 1944. This aircraft appears to be in the tricolour scheme. Apparently, a mixed bag of paint schemes was sported by the squadron, as other photographs of the squadron's aeroplanes taken about the same time show them in overall glossy blue. (*National Archives 80-G-243412*)

Gambier Bay being straddled by large calibre near misses during the battle. In the original print, a Japanese cruiser can just be seen on the horizon. (*National Archives 80-G-287502*)

Gambier Bay making smoke during the battle. (*National Archives 80-G-288145*)

One of VC-10's FM-2s at Tacloban airfield.
(*USAF 55474 AC*)

Fanshaw Bay (CVE-70) displaying the
Measure 14 camouflage carried by *Gambier
Bay* prior to being repainted in Measure
32/15a. Unlike *Gambier Bay*, she carried her
flight deck number aft. (*National Archives
80-G-214084*)

Kalinin Bay (CVE-68) took a number of hits during the action off Samar. *Gambier Bay* suffered similar flight deck damage. (*National Archives 80-G-270510*)

St. Lo (CVE-63) was sunk several hours after *Gambier Bay*, although her loss was attributed to a kamikaze. She is shown here in April 1944. (*National Archives* 80-G-47028)

St. Lo burning after the second explosion, 25 October 1944. (*National Archives* 80-G-270511)

Gambier Bay's radar suite comprised YE (top), SG (just below the YE), and SK (large antenna). (*National Archives 80-G-218332*)

Ltjg O E Wheeler bringing his TBM-1C
aboard *Gambier Bay* for his 1000th landing.
(*National Archives 80-G-243433*)

CVE catwalks provided storage for fire hoses and other gear. (*National Archives 80-G-289812*)

The hangar deck of a *Casablanca* class CVE was not overly spacious, but provided sufficient storage and repair space for the small air units carried. (*National Archives 80-G-298057*)

Gambier Bay and her sisters normally carried twenty 20mm Oerlikons in tubs on either side of the gallery deck. (*National Archives 80-G-262716*)

The mast was a relatively complex structure supporting radar, searchlights, and various other electronic gear. (*National Archives 80-G-262708*)

The Drawings

A General arrangement

A1   OUTBOARD PROFILE
     (1/384 scale)

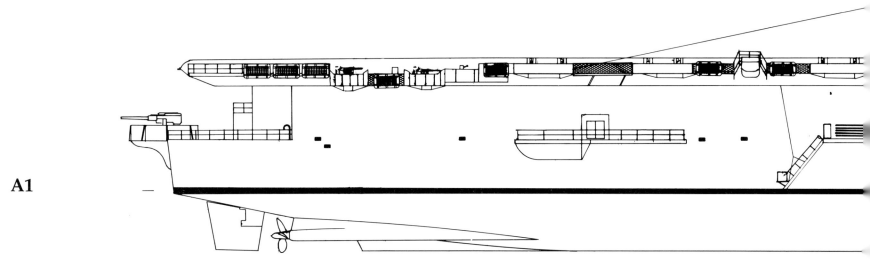

A1

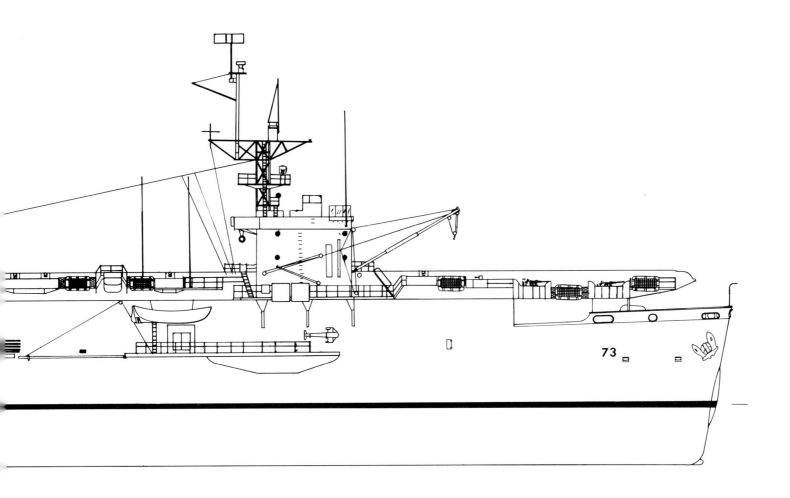

73

A General arrangement

A2   INBOARD PROFILE (1/384 scale)

1	Ammunition handling	10	Duct
2	Catapult machinery room	11	Aviation belting & belt link stowage
3	Head	12	Oxygen room
4	Navigation officer's stateroom	13	Wardroom/stateroom
5	Passage	14	Elevator machinery room
6	Flight crew lockers	15	Elevator
7	Ready room	16	Motion picture projection room
8	Photo lab	17	Raincoat locker
9	IC room & emergency switchboard	18	Hangar

19	Master at arms office
20	Torpedo repair shop
21	Aviation shop
22	Bosun's stores
23	Chain locker
24	CPO head
25	CPO berthing
26	Carpenter's shop
27	Elevator pit

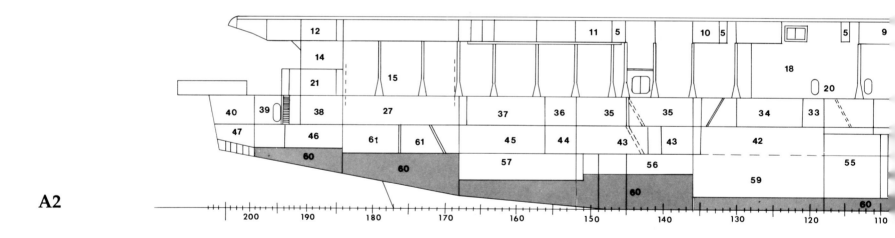

A2

28	Hospital space	37	Crew's mess & bomb handling	46	Steering gear flat	55	Fresh water tank
29	Degaussing room	38	Crew's head	47	Pyrotechnics locker	56	Aircraft ammunition stowage
30	Executive officer's office	39	Capstan room	48	Fuel oil or salt water ballast	57	Bomb stowage
31	Navigation & gunnery office	40	Laundry	49	Dry provision stores	58	Forward engine & boiler room
32	Wardroom mess & recreation room	41	Gas pump room	50	Incendiary stowage	59	Aft engine & boiler room
33	Ship's service stores	42	Machinery flat	51	20mm & 40mm magazine	60	Fuel oil tanks
34	Crew mess & parachute packing	43	Refrigerator & dry stores	52	Aviation gas tanks	61	Crew berthing
35	Crew's galley	44	Bomb vanes	53	GSK & SD stores		
36	Main distribution panel room	45	Aviation stores	54	Lube oil tank		

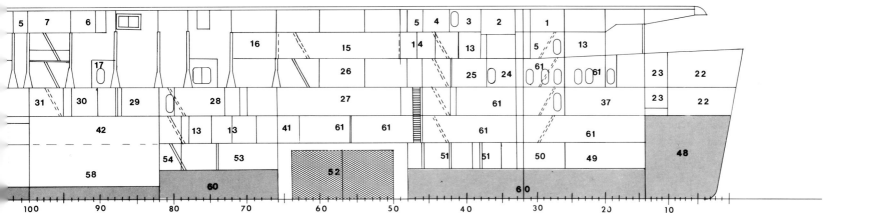

A General arrangement

A3   TRANSVERSE SECTIONS
       (1/384 scale)

A3/1   Frame 184 looking aft

1   Fan room
2   Passage
3   Elevator machinery
4   Aviation shop
5   Passage
6   Crew shower
7   Crew head
8   5in powder stowage
9   Steering gear platform
10   Fuel oil tank

A3/2   Frame 168 looking aft

1   Radar room
2   Hangar
3   Crew's berthing
4   Elevator pit
5   Fuel oil tank

A3/3   Frame 136 looking aft

1   Flight deck gear & repair
2   Hangar
3   Vegetable preparation room
4   Crew's galley
5   Dry provisions
6   Butcher's shop
7   Clothing & small stores
8   Stowage
9   Aircraft ammunition stowage
10   Void
11   Shaft
12   Fuel oil tank

A3/1

A3/2

A3/3

A3/4 *Frame 118 looking aft/Frame 100*
looking forward

1   Hangar
2   Platform
3   Ship's store
4   Crew's mess & parachute packing
5   Navigation & gunnery officers'
    stores
6   Passage
7   Chaplain's office
8   Cleaning gear locker
9   Machinery flat
10 Aft engine & boiler room
11 Forward engine & boiler room
12 Fuel oil tank

A3/5 *Frame 66 looking forward*

1   Hangar
2   Lobby
3   Engineer's stateroom
4   Aviation ready isssue
5   Elevator pit
6   Passage
7   Medical stores
8   Gas pump room
9   Crew's berthing
10 Cofferdam

A3/6 *Frame 48 looking forward*

1   Passage
2   Elevator machinery room
3   Lobby
4   Wardroom/stateroom
5   Passage
6   CPO berthing
7   20mm & 40mm magazine
8   Fuel oil tank

A3/7 *Frame 14 looking forward*

1   Chain locker
2   Void
3   Fuel oil or salt water ballast

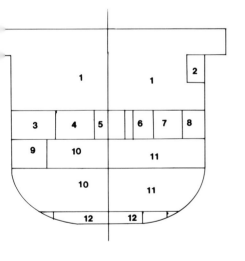

A3/4

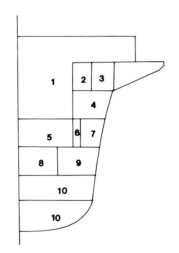

A3/5

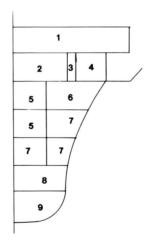

A3/6

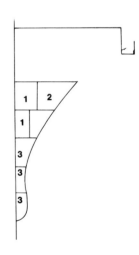

A3/7

A General arrangement

A4   FLIGHT DECK(1/384 scale)
1   40mm position
2   MK51 director
3   20mm position
4   Ramp
5   H2-1 catapult
6   Elevator
7   LSO platform
8   Expansion joint
9   Arresting gear
10   Crash barrier
11   Sky lookout

A4

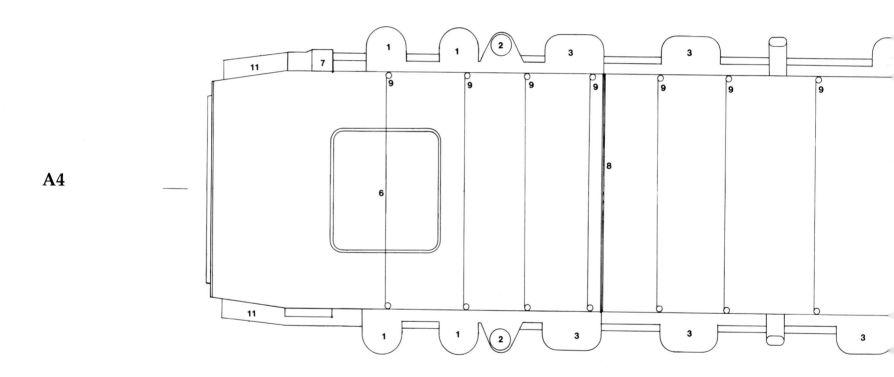

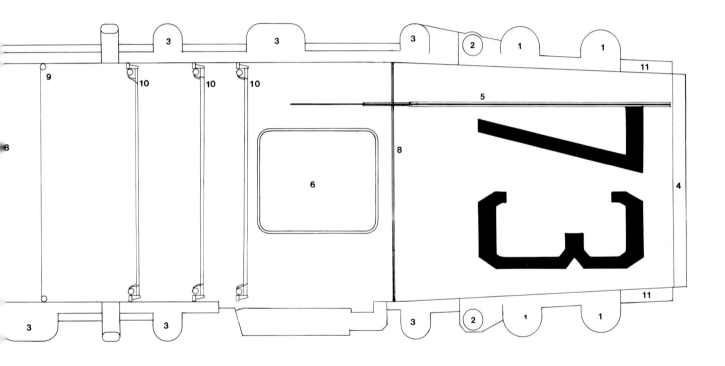

A General arrangement

A5   ISLAND (1/384 scale)

A5/1   Inboard profile

1   Steering station
2   Lobby
3   Chart room
4   Passage
5   Captain's sea cabin
6   Navigator's sea cabin
7   Chart room
8   Radio message room
9   RDF room

A5/2   Gunnery control

1   Captain's battle station
2   Passage
3   Gunnery Officer's station
4   Tower base
5   Venturi
6   Vertical ladder

A5/3   Navigating bridge

1   Steering station
2   Passage
3   Chart room

A5/3

A5/4   SG radar level

A5/4

A5/5   SK radar level

A5/5

A5/6   Signal yard arm level

A5/6

A5/7   24in searchlight level

A5/7

A5/8   12in signal light level

A5/8

A5/1

A5/2

A6   GALLERY DECK (1/384 scale)

1   40mm ready service
2   Ammunition hoist
3   Radar room
4   Head
5   Air officer's stateroom
6   Navigation officer's stateroom
7   Gunnery officer's stateroom
8   Catapult officer's stores
9   Lobby
10 Aero lab

11 Pilot balloon room
12 Wardroom stores
13 20mm ready service/clipping room
14 Passage
15 Executive officer's stateroom
16 Air intelligence
17 Radio communications
18 Crew shelter
19 Radio central
20 Coding room

21 Printing and developing
22 Squadron ready room
23 Parachute stowage
24 Air intake
25 Battery room
26 IC room & emergency switchboard
27 Squadron office
28 Battery charging station
29 Fan room
30 Aviation belt & belt link stowage

A6

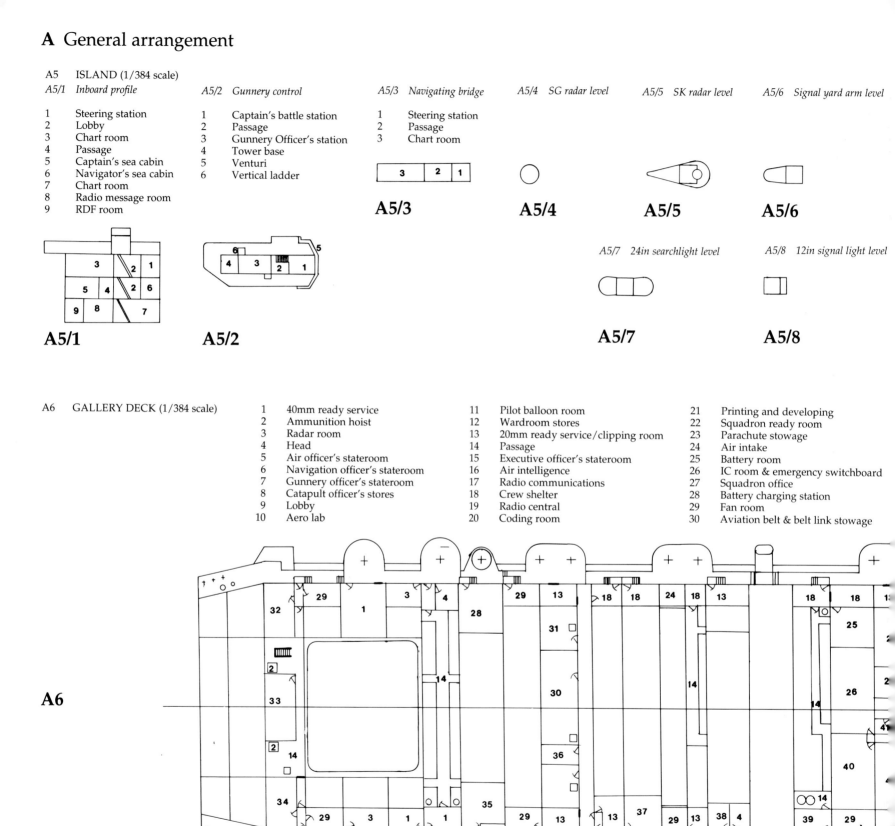

60

A5/9 Railings at the gallery deck level
(1/72 scale)

1 Flag bags
2 Chain
3 Pipe rail
4 Inclined ladder
5 Island

A5/9

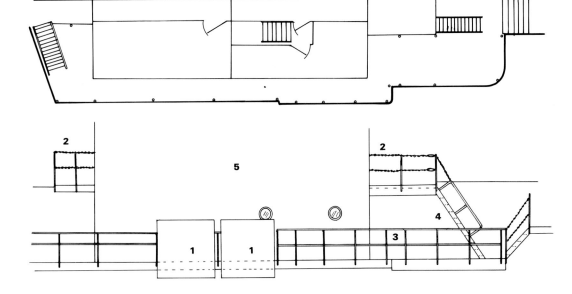

31 Squadron gear locker	41 Stock room and camera stowage	51 Radar control	60 Captain's stateroom
32 CO_2 transfer room	42 Finishing room	52 Radar plot	61 Navigator's store
33 Oxygen transfer room	43 Air department office	53 Radio message room	62 Air plot
34 Aviation stores & arresting gear spares	44 Officer's head	54 Chartroom	63 Catapult machinery room
35 Arresting gear repair shop	45 Lobby	55 Conflagration locker	64 Resistor room
36 Bombsight stowage	46 Flight crew locker	56 Captain's pantry	65 Junior officers' bunk room
37 Flight deck gear & repair	47 Squadron service room	57 Captain's cabin	66 Sky lookouts
38 Hangar deck light control	48 Radio transmitter room	58 Captain's stores	
39 Flight deck light control	49 Radar transmitter room	59 Captain's bath	
40 Flight crew locker room	50 Radio direction finder room		

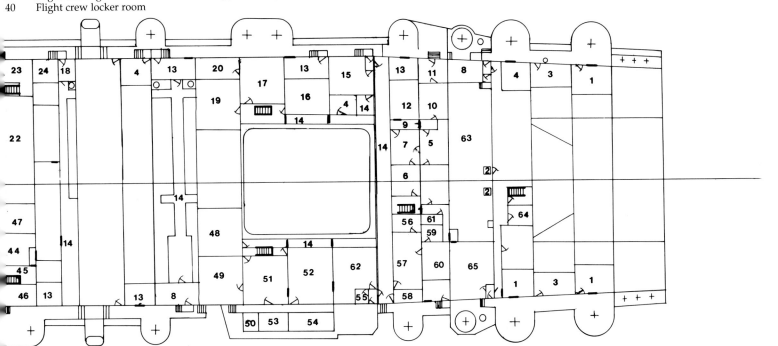

A General arrangement

A7   UPPER DECK (1/384 scale)

1	Wardroom	12	Lobby
2	Passage	13	Ship's radio storage
3	Ammunition hoist	14	Platform
4	Squadron command room	15	Top of Master at Arms office
5	Steam room	16	Top of torpedo repair shop
6	Aviators' conditioning room	17	Boiler room uptake
7	Elevator machinery room	18	Machine-gun cleaning flat
8	Shower space	19	Integrity and conflagration station
9	Aircraft radio repair and stowage	20	Linen locker
10	Film stowage locker	21	Engineers' storeroom
11	Motion projector room	22	Fan room

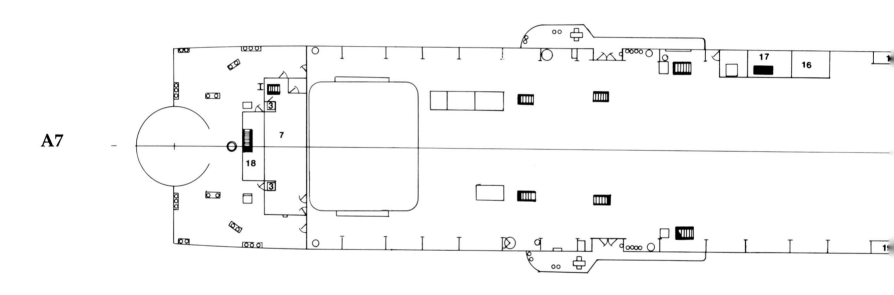

A7

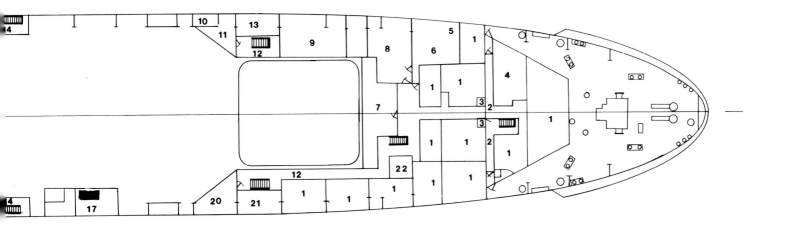

A General arrangement

A8   HANGAR DECK (1/384 scale)

1	Bosun's stores	12	Ammunition hoist	23	Reserve
2	Chain locker	13	Carpenter and pipe-fitter shop	24	Aviation ready issue
3	Void	14	CPO berthing	25	Hangar deck gear
4	Parachute repair & canvas shop	15	Plate & bar stowage	26	Deck gear
5	Lamp room	16	Passage	27	Fan room
6	Paint room	17	Elevator pit	28	Lucky bag
7	Wardroom stores	18	Raincoat locker	29	Resistor room
8	Reg. Pubs. locker	19	Master at Arms office	30	Cell
9	CPO showers	20	Torpedo repair and tool room	31	Brig
10	Escape trunk	21	Boiler uptake		
11	CPO wardroom and head	22	Deck office		

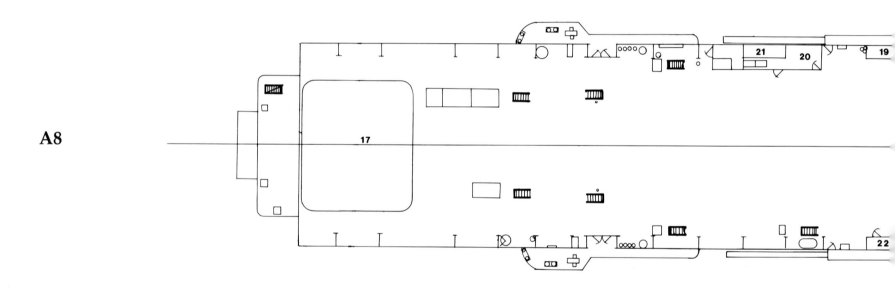

A8

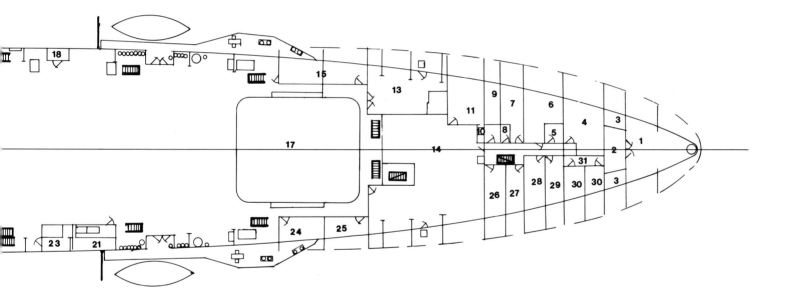

A General arrangement

A9   SECOND DECK (1/384 scale)

1   Crews' water closet
2   Passage
3   Crew's shower room
4   Ammunition hoist
5   Escape trunk
6   Elevator pit
7   Acid locker
8   Deck locker
9   Isolation ward
10 Diet pantry
11 Medical officer's stateroom

12 Head
13 Officers' head
14 Dentist's head
15 Linen locker
16 Sick bay
17 Supply officer's stores
18 Disbursing office
19 Captain's office
20 1st Lieutenant & damage control office
21 Wardroom mess and recreation room

22 Officers' galley
23 Main issue room
24 Engineer's stowage
25 Machinery room
26 Ship's service store
27 Provision issue room
28 Bakery
29 Bread room
30 Crew mess & bomb handling
31 Cot locker
32 Crew's berthing

33 Cleaning gear locker
34 Barber shop
35 Tailor shop
36 Mess attendants' head
37 Post office
38 Mess attendants' berthing
39 Capstan room
40 Laundry
41 Resistor room
42 Issue room
43 Linen room

A9

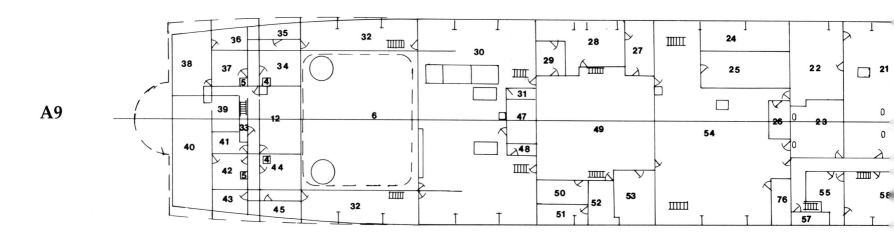

44	Crew shower	55	CPO pantry	66	Dispensary & office
45	Soiled linen room	56	Navigation and gunnery office	67	X-ray & surgical dressing
46	Repair party locker	57	CPO stores	68	Prophylaxis room
47	Main distribution panel room	58	CPO mess	69	Sterilising & scrub room
48	Hammock locker	59	Executive officer's office	70	Operating room
49	Crew's galley	60	Degaussing room	71	Medical stores
50	Scullery	61	Cleaning gear locker	72	Alcohol locker
51	Trash room	62	Engineer's stowage	73	Crew's locker room
52	Garbage disposal room	63	Medical locker	74	Chain locker
53	Vegetable preparation room	64	Dark room	75	Bosun's stores
54	Crew's mess and parachute packing	65	Lobby	76	Ship's store

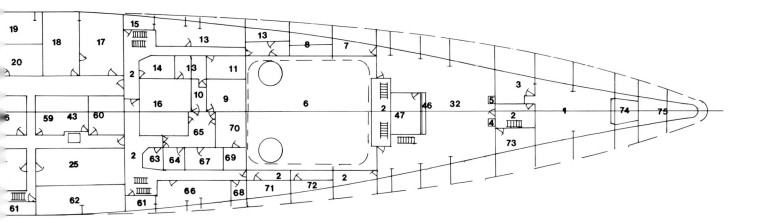

A General arrangement

1	Salt water ballast	13	Generator room	25	Pyrotechnic stowage	37	Kerosene locker
2	Crew berthing	14	Milk preparation	26	Steering gear platform	38	Engineer's locker
3	Escape trunk	15	Dairy	27	5in projectile stowage	39	Electrical workshop
4	Ammunition hoist	16	Fruit	28	5in powder stowage	40	Gyro room
5	Wardroom	17	Ice	29	Aircraft ammunition	41	Upper part forward engine & boiler room
6	Gas pump room	18	Fresh water settling tank	30	Dry provision		
7	Inert gas	19	Vegetables	31	Butcher shop	42	Linen locker
8	Cleaning gear locker	20	Meat	32	Machinery flat	43	Machine-gun repair
9	Passage	21	Dummy drill material	33	Upper part aft engine & boiler room		
10	Aviation armoury	22	Bomb vanes	34	Fresh water tank		
11	Ship's armoury	23	Aviation stores	35	CO_2 room		
12	Fuel oil settling tank	24	20mm & 40mm ammunition stowage	36	Spare parts stowage		

A10

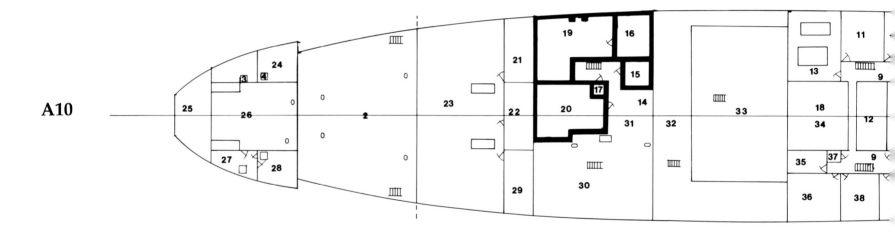

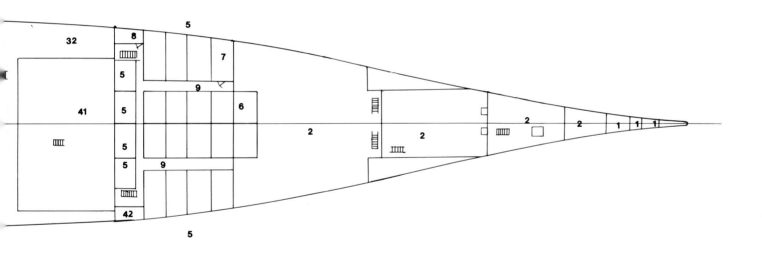

32

8

5

41

5

5

5

5

42

5

7

9

6

9

5

2

2

2

2

2

1

1

1

A General arrangement

A11   TANK TOP (1/384 scale)

1 Salt water ballast	9 Forward engine & boiler room	17 Ordnance stores	25 Captain's store stowage
2 Incendiary bomb magazine	10 Fuel oil settling tank	18 Passage	26 C & R stores
3 Ammunition hoist	11 Machine shop	19 Aircraft ammunition stowage	27 Lube oil
4 Escape trunk	12 Fresh water tank	20 Bomb stowage	28 GSK & SD stores
5 Handling room	13 Shaft alley flat	21 Ship's service store stowage	29 Bomb fuse magazine
6 Aviation gas tank	14 Diesel oil	22 Clothing & small stores issue room	30 Dry provision stores
7 Cofferdam	15 Aft engine & boiler room	23 Clothing & small bulk stores	31 20mm & 40mm magazine
8 Lube oil	16 Chemical warfare equipment	24 Engineer's store & stock issue room	32 Fuel oil tank

A11

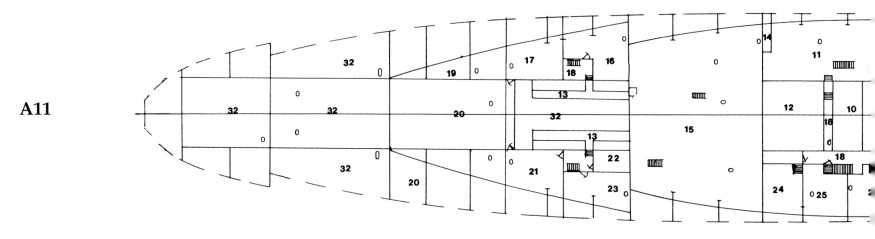

A12   DOUBLE BOTTOM (1/384 scale)

1   Salt water ballast
2   Fuel oil tank
3   Cofferdam
4   Aviation gas tank
5   Water tank
6   Void
7   Sump tank
8   Fathometer

A12

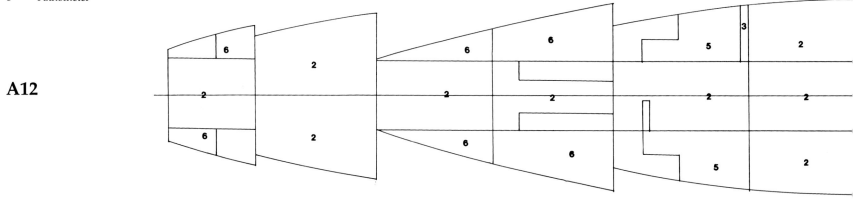

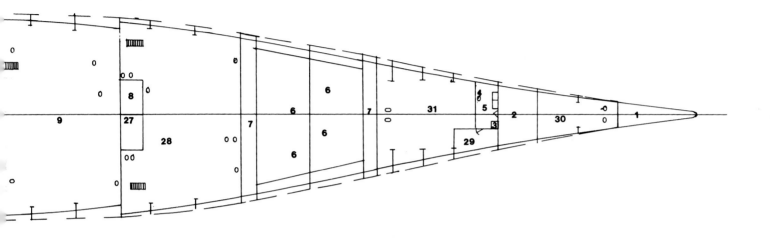

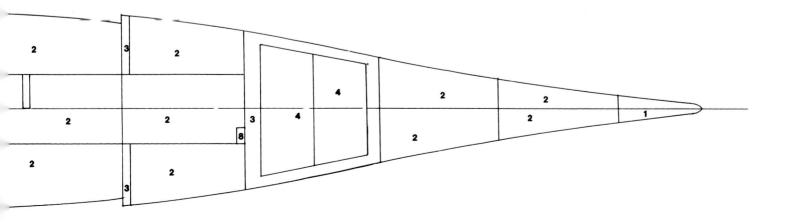

71

A General arrangement

A13   DETAILS FORWARD (1/384 scale)

1	Davit	12	26ft motor whaleboat	17	TCE antenna	22	RDF
2	Paravane chain bracket	13	Boat boom	18	SK radar antenna	23	TDE/TBK antenna
3	Double roller chock	14	Uptake	19	SG radar antenna	24	TBL antenna
4	Triple roller chock	15	Flag bag	20	YE antanna	25	20mm mount
5	Sky lookout	16	Portable windscreen	21	TBS antenna	26	24in searchlight
6	40mm mount						
7	MK51 director						
8	Aircraft/cargo boom						
9	Island support girder						
10	Paravene in stowed position						
11	Forward sponson						

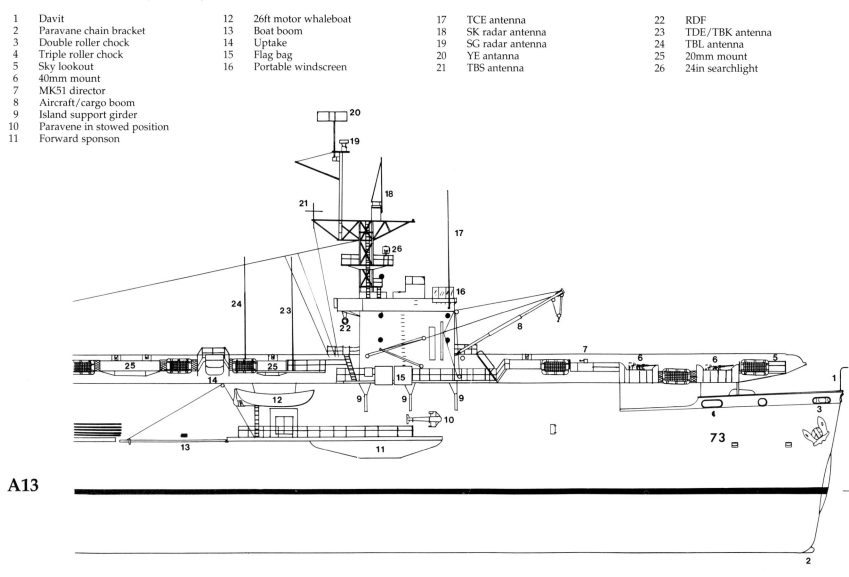

A13

A14   DETAILS AFT (1/384 scale)

1   5in/38 mount
2   40mm mount
3   MK51 director
4   20mm mount
5   Uptake
6   Refuelling hoses
7   Accommodation ladder
8   Freeing port
9   Gooseneck vent
10   Sky lookout

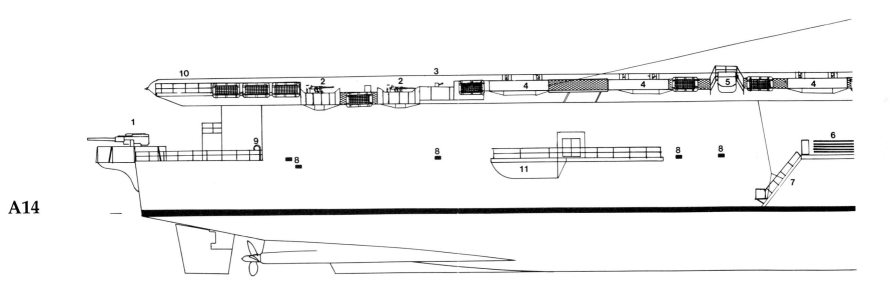

A14

B Lines and constructional details

B1   SHEER DRAFT (1/384 scale)

B1

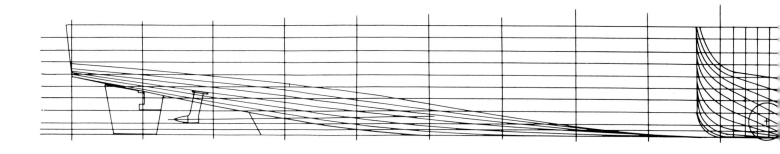

B2   PLAN VIEW (1/384 scale)

B2

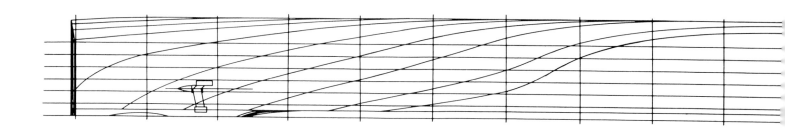

B3   STEM CASTING (1/64 scale)

B3

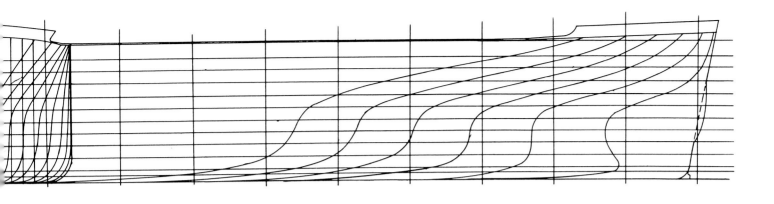

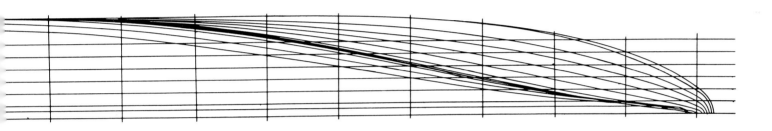

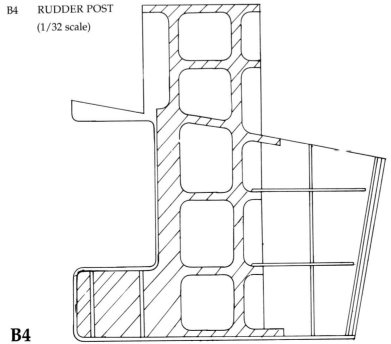

B4   RUDDER POST
(1/32 scale)

B4

B Lines and constructional details

B5/1   Bow

1   20.4# STS
2   25.5# STS
3   35.6# STS
4   30.6# STS
5   22.95# STS

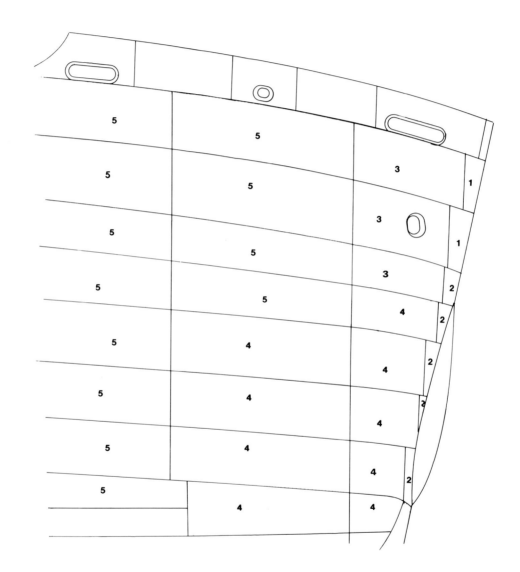

B5/1

B5/2   *Stern*

1   20.4# STS
2   25.5# STS
3   35.6# STS
4   30.6# STS
5   22.95# STS
6   17.85# STS

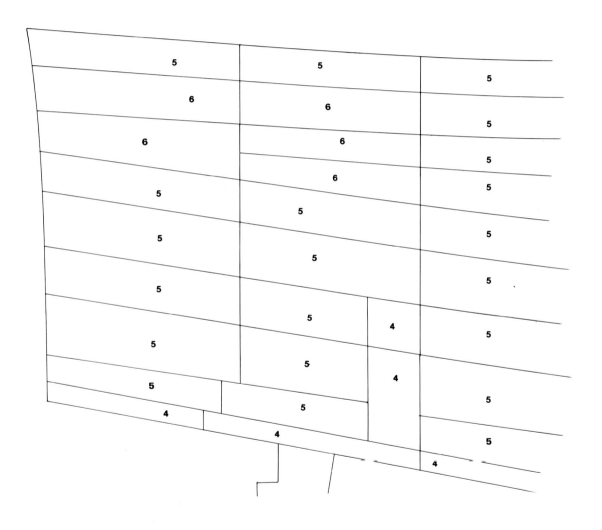

B5/2

B Lines and constructional details

B6 PROPELLOR SHAFT STRUTS
(1/32 scale)

B6/1   *Forward strut*

B6/2   *Main strut side view*

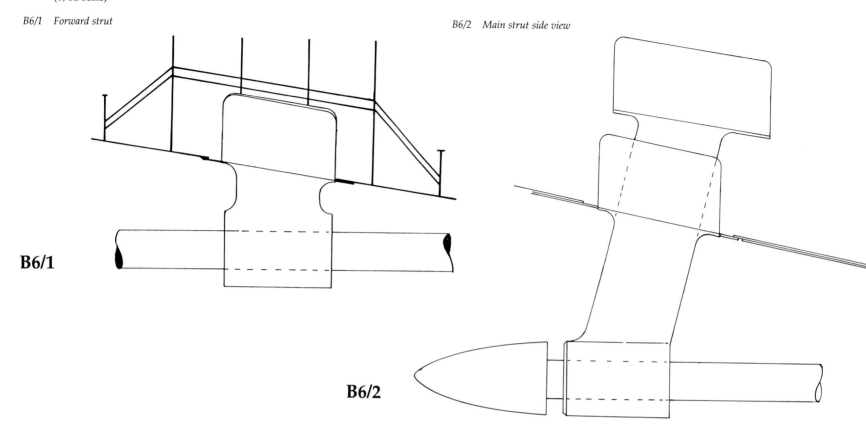

B6/1

B6/2

B6/3   *Main strut front view*

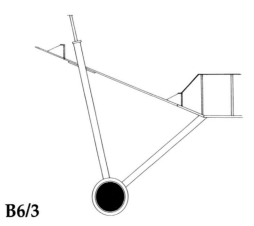

B6/3

B7   PROPELLOR SHAFT HOUSING
      LINES (no scale)

B8   RUDDER/SHAFT
      ARRANGEMENT (1/96 scale)

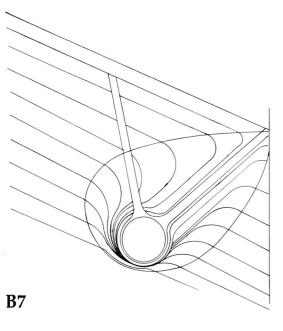

B7

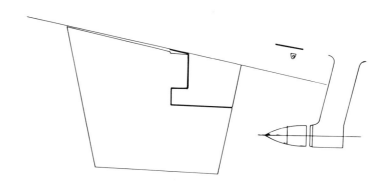

B8

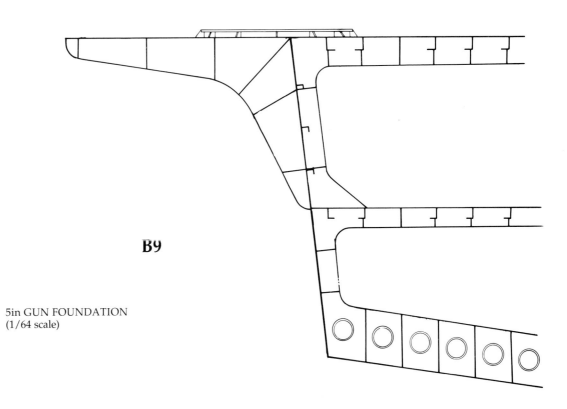

B9

B9   5in GUN FOUNDATION
      (1/64 scale)

B10   5in GUNSHIELD FRAMING
        (1/64 scale)

B10

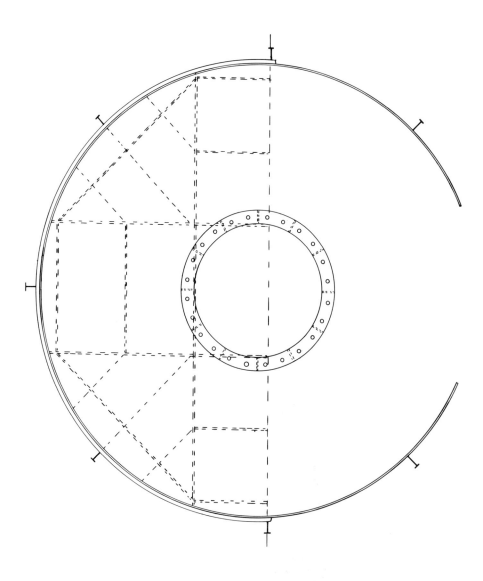

B11   SPONSON FRAMING (1/72 scale)

B11/1 Forward

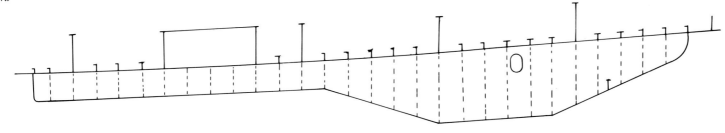

B11/1

B11/2 Midships

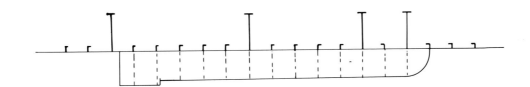

B11/2

B11/3 Aft

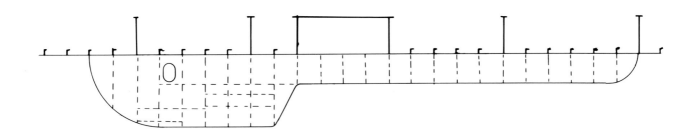

B11/3

B12   20MM PLATFORM (1/72 scale)

1   20# STS plating
2   7.65# CR plating
3   Inclined ladder

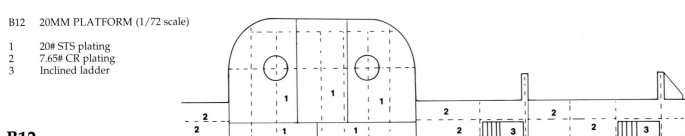

B12

C Machinery

C1 SECTION THROUGH
MACHINERY SERVICES
(1/192 scale)

C1/1 Frame 126 looking forward

1   Boiler
2   Forward engine shaft
3   Main feed pump
4   Aft engine
5   Main condenser
6   Main condensate pump
7   Main circulation pump

C2 SECTION THROUGH UNIFLOW
ENGINE (no scale)

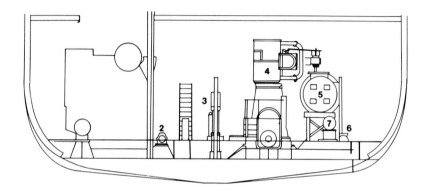

C1/1

C1/2 Frame 100 looking aft

1   Boiler
2   Main feed pump
3   Auxiliary condenser
4   Auxiliary circulation pump
5   Main condenser
6   Aft engine
7   Feed water settling tank
8   Fuel oil service pump

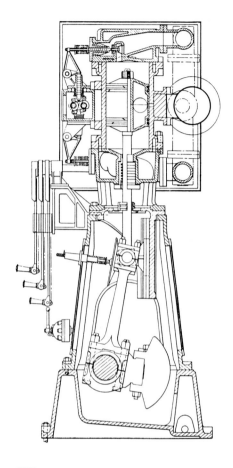

C2

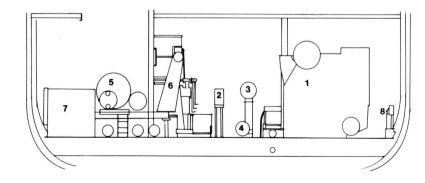

C1/2

D Rig

D1   SKI RADAR (1/128 scale)

D1/1 Framework

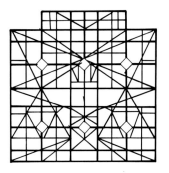

D1/1

D1/2 Dipoles

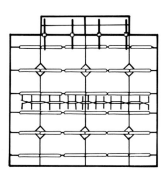

D1/2

D1/3 Reflecting dipoles

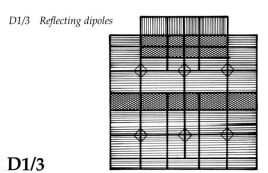

D1/3

D2   SG RADAR (1/48 scale)

D2/1 SG RADAR PLATFORM

1   YE drive shaft
2   Topmast
3   SG radar drive
4   SG platform
5   YE drive motor
6   Vertical ladder
7   Vertical fighting lights
8   Battle ensign gaff

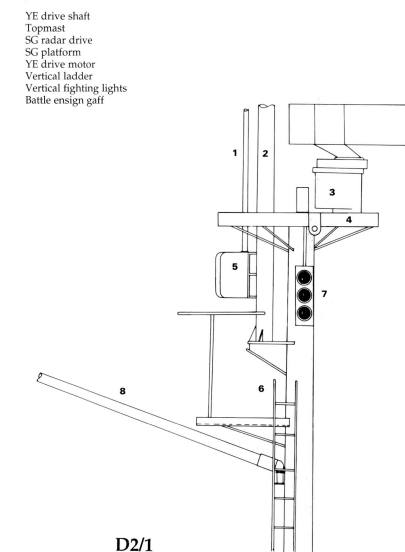

D2/1

D Rig

D3   TOWER (1/96 scale)

D3/1 *Lower tower and island, looking forward*

1   Fighting lights
2   RDF loop
3   Signal halyards
4   Searchlight platform
5   Radar platform

D3/2 *Tower at searchlight level*

1   24in searchlight platform
2   12in signal light platform
3   Vertical ladder
4   Ship's bell

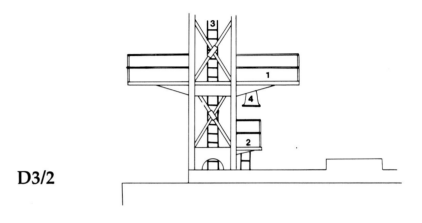

D3/2

D3/3 *24in searchlight platform*

1   Searchlight base
2   Opening
3   Vertical ladder

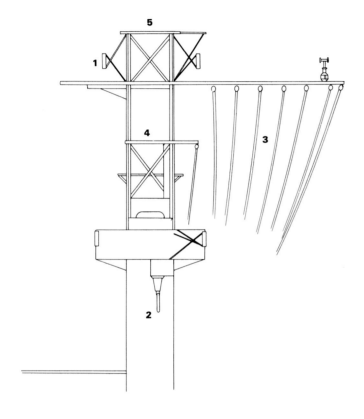

D3/1

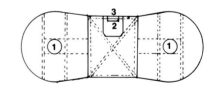

D3/3

D3/4 Signal yard platform

1   Reproducer base
2   Opening
3   Vertical ladder

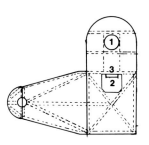

D3/4

D3/5 Signal yardarm

1   Tower
2   Handrail
3   BN antenna
4   Anemometer
5   Blinker lamp
6   Foot rope
7   Cleat
8   Foot rope and bracket
9   Stay

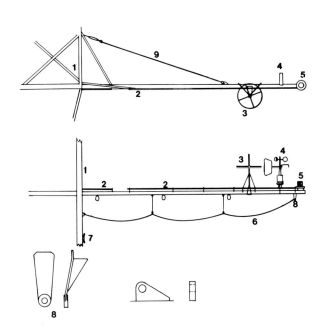

D3/5

D4   VERTICAL FIGHTING LIGHTS
      ON SUPERSTRUCTURE
      (1/96 scale)

D4/1 Outboard view

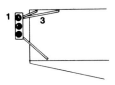

D4/1

D4/2 Plan and side views

1   Fighting lights
2   Reproducer
3   Struts
4   Reproducer brackets

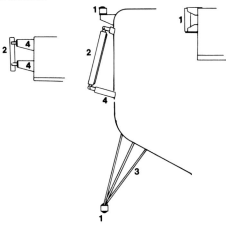

D4/2

E Armament

E1   5in/38 GENERAL
      ARRANGEMENT (1/48 scale)

(Numbers apply to all views)

E1/1   *Port elevation*

E1/2   *Starboard elevation*

E1/3   *Front view*

E1/4   *Top view*

1   Barrel
2   Housing
3   Carriage
4   Slide
5   Stand
6   Platform
7   Sight
8   Elevating gear
9   Training gear
10   Fuse setting gear
11   Gun train indicator
12   Gun elevation indicator
13   Fuse setting indicator
14   Telescopes

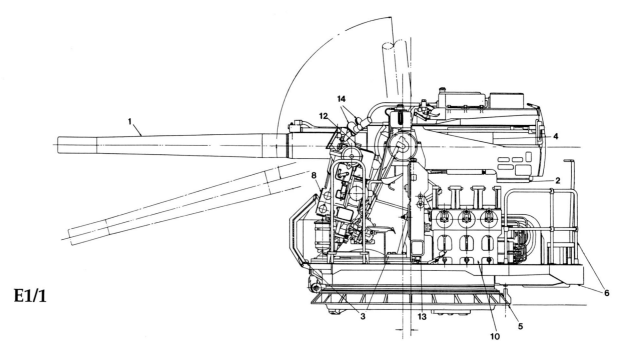

E1/1

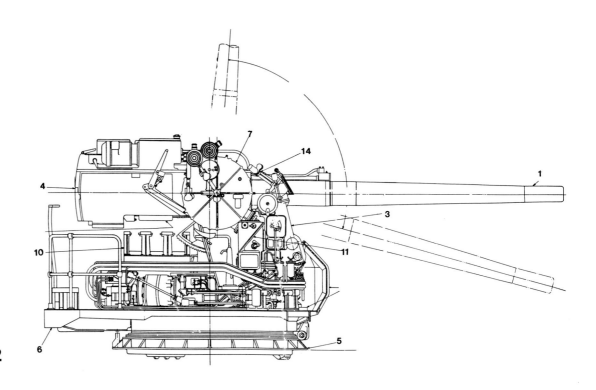

E1/2

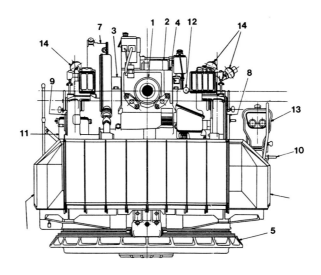

E1/3

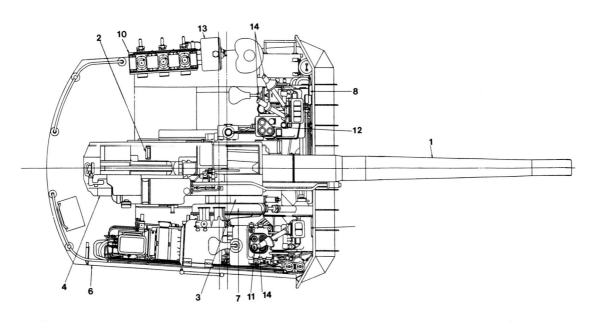

E1/4

E Armament

E2 5in/38 MK12 RAMMER CONTROLS (no scale)

1 Barrel
2 Operating lever
3 Rammer gear housing
4 Rammer motor
5 Cam plate
6 Spade release lever
7 Space
8 Case stop
9 Carriage

E3 STAND AND CARRIAGE FOR 5in/38 (no scale)

1 Gun carriage
2 Trunnion bearing
3 Depression stop
4 Elevation stop
5 Centre plate
6 Training pinion gear housing
7 Platform

E5 BREECH BLOCK AND EXTRACTORS, 5in/38 (no scale)

1 Lip
2 Firing pin
3 Pallet
4 Bearing block ways
5 Outer lug
6 Shelf
7 Seal

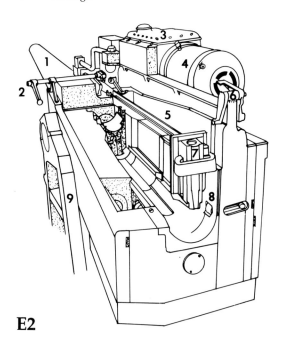

E2

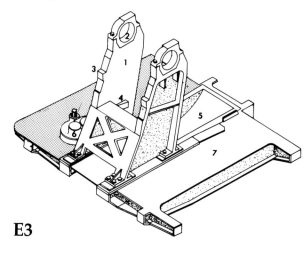

E3

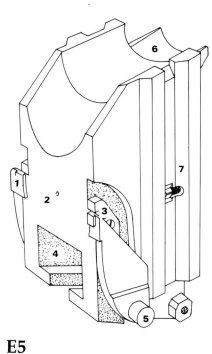

E5

E4 BREECH HAND OPERATING LEVER DETAILS, 5in/38 (no scale)

1 Slide
2 Rammer gear housing
3 Rammer gear housing
4 Hand operating lever
5 Lever catch
6 Connecting link
7 Elevating arc

E6 5in/38 SHELL, ANTI-AIRCRAFT, COMMON (1/24 scale)

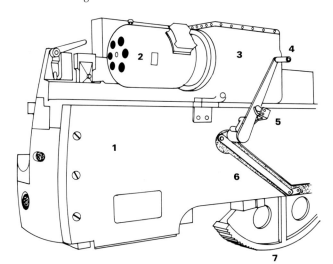

E4

E6

E7   TWIN 40MM MK1 MOUNT
      (1/32 scale)

E7/1   Top View

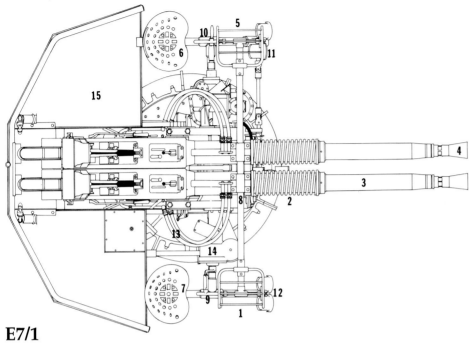

E7/1

E7/2   Starboard elevation

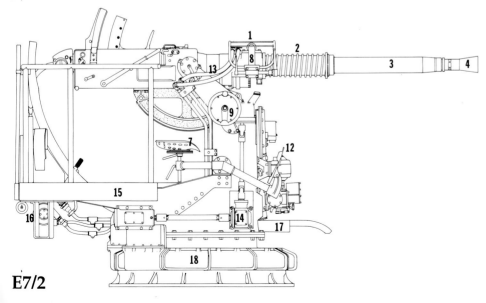

E7/2

E7/3   Front view

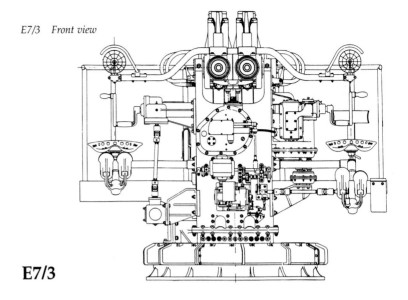

E7/3

E7/4   Rear view

1   Open sight for trainer
2   Spring
3   Barrel
4   Flash guard
5   Open sight for pointer
6   Pointer's seat
7   Trainer's seat
8   Sight bar
9   Training handwheel
10   Pointing handwheel
11   Firing pedal
12   Footrests
13   Hydraulic lines
14   Training gear
15   Platform
16   Cooling pump
17   Shell chute
18   Base

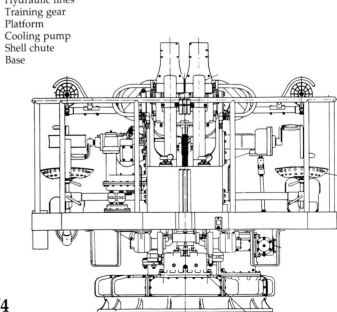

E7/4

E Armament

E8 40MM RING SIGHT

E8/1 Front view

F8/2 Side view

E8/1

E8/2

E9 40MM SIGHT BAR COMPLETE
(1/32 scale)

E9

E10 40MM SLIDE AND LOADER ARRANGEMENT (no scale)

1　Recoil cylinder
2　Recoil piston rod mount
3　Firing plunger
4　Trunnion
5　Top door
6　Side door
7　Front guide
8　Loader guide and pawls
9　Rear guide
10　Firing selector lever
11　Case deflector

E10

E11 LOADER, 40MM (no scale)

1　Front guide
2　Right loader frame
3　Rear guide
4　Slide
5　Stop pawls
6　Feed pawls
7　Star wheel
8　Star wheel catch
9　Rammer tray

E11

E12 RAMMER TRAY, 40MM (no scale)

1　Securing bolt hole
2　Rammer tray pawl
3　Guide for feed pawl roller
4　Rammer lever
5　Rammer shoe guide
6　Rammer lever slot

E12

E13   BREECH MECHANISM, 40MM
        (no scale)

1   Housing
2   Gun barrel catch control arm
3   Breech block
4   Operating spring case
5   Rammer tray
6   Outer cocking lever
7   Extractor shaft hole
8   Recoil piston rod bolt hole
9   Roller
10   Crankshaft

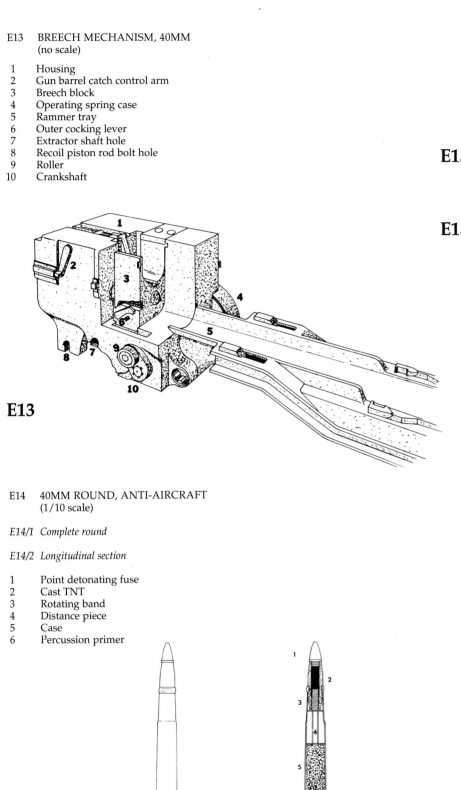

E13

E14   40MM ROUND, ANTI-AIRCRAFT
        (1/10 scale)

E14/1 Complete round

E14/2 Longitudinal section

1   Point detonating fuse
2   Cast TNT
3   Rotating band
4   Distance piece
5   Case
6   Percussion primer

E14/1   **E14/2**

E15   20MM GUN (1/32 scale)

E15/1 Elevation

E15/2 Top view

E15/1
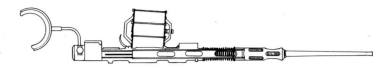

E15/2
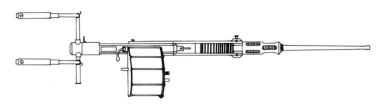

E16   20MM MOUNT MK4 (1/32 scale)

E16/1 Elevation, with mount for MK14
        gunsight

E16/2 Elevation, showing mount at maximum
        height

E16/3 Top view

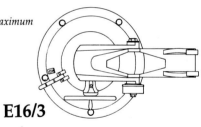
E16/3

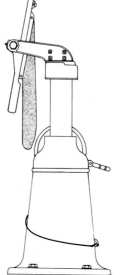
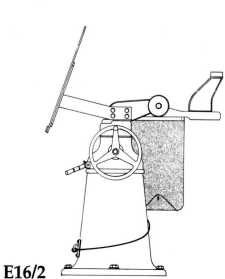

E16/1   **E16/2**

E Armament

E17 GUN SHIELD FOR 20MM

1 Shield
2 Rear brace carriage bolts
3 Tie bar

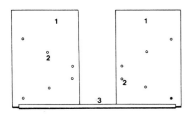

E17

E18 20MM AMMUNITION (1/2 scale)

E18/1 Complete round, anti-aircraft

E18/2 Longitudinal section, anti-aircraft round

E18/3 Longitudinal section, HET

E18/4 Longitudinal section, HET

E18/5 Longitudinal section, armour-piercing

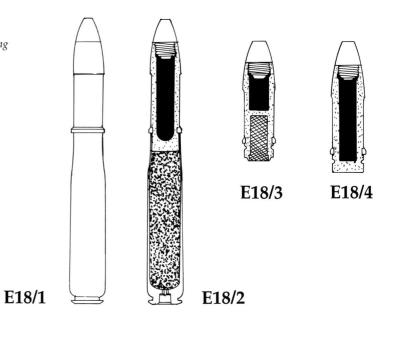

E18/1   **E18/2**   **E18/3**   **E18/4**   **E18/5**

E19 MK51 DIRECTOR (1/32 scale)

E19/1 Rear view

1 Base
2 Director handles
3 Air pump
4 Counterbalance weights

E19/2 Side elevation

1 Air pump
2 Base
3 Director handle with firing key
4 Range rate setter
5 Range setter
6 Air pressure gauge
7 Counterbalance weight

E19/3 Plan view

1 Air pump
2 Director handles
3 Elevation detent
4 Range rate setter
5 Range setter
6 Access to wind syncro
7 Counterbalance weight

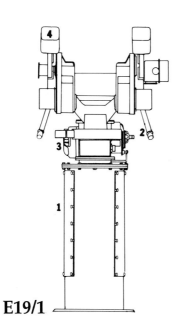

E19/1

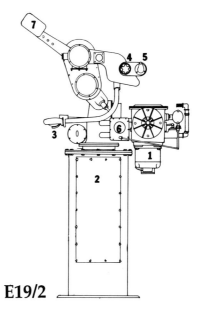

E19/2

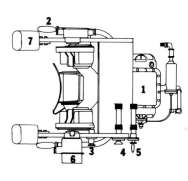

E19/3

F Fittings

F1   UPPER DECK FITTINGS
       (1/384 scale)

1   Triple roller chocks
2   Double roller chocks
3   Hawse pipes
4   Hatch
5   14in bitt
6   12in bitt
7   Anchor winch

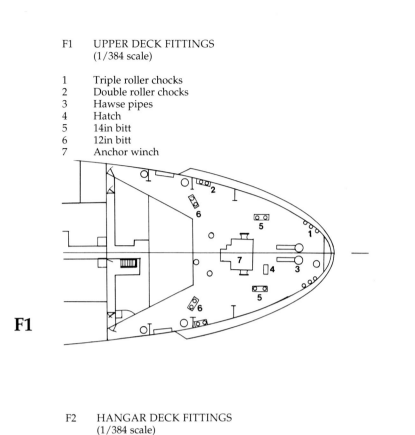

F1

F2   HANGAR DECK FITTINGS
       (1/384 scale)

1   Triple roller chocks
2   Double roller chocks
3   5in gun mount
4   Capstan
5   14in bitt
6   12in bitt
7   Hawser real
8   Watertight escape hatch
9   Cane fenders
10   Aircraft propellers
11   Winch
12   Fuel oil fills
13   Gas hose
14   Hatch

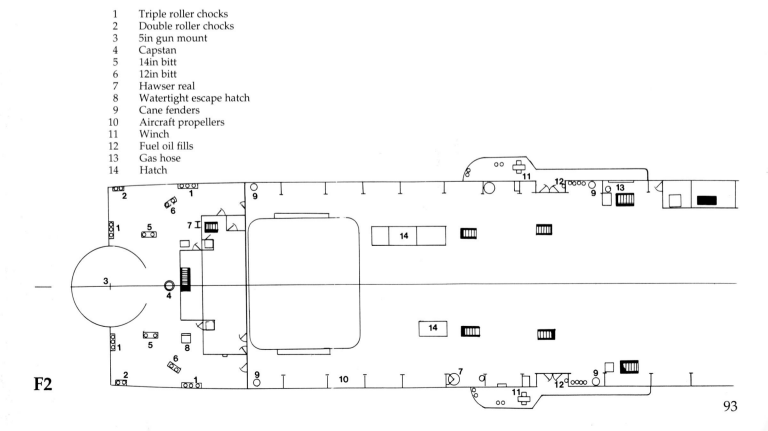

F2

F Fittings

F3   WATERTIGHT DOORS

F3/1   Typical door (no scale)

1   Coaming
2   Dog
3   Hinge
4   Handle

F3/2   Dog arrangement (no scale)

F3/3   Alternate dog arrangement

F3/4   Type B catch for scuttles and hatches

F3/5   Hinge arrangement

F3/6   Small double hatch (1/48 scale)

F3/7   Large double hatch (1/48 scale)

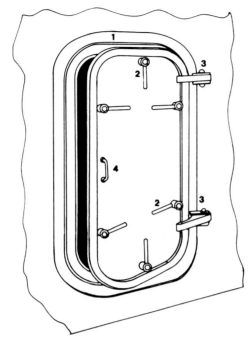

F3/1

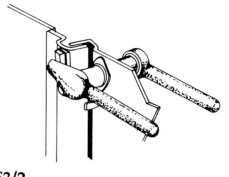

F3/2

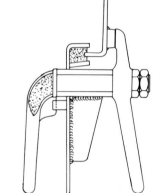

F3/3

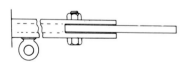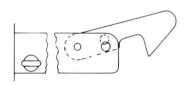

F3/4

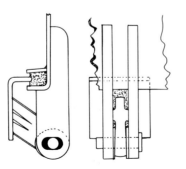

F3/5

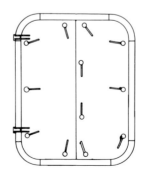

F3/6

F3/7

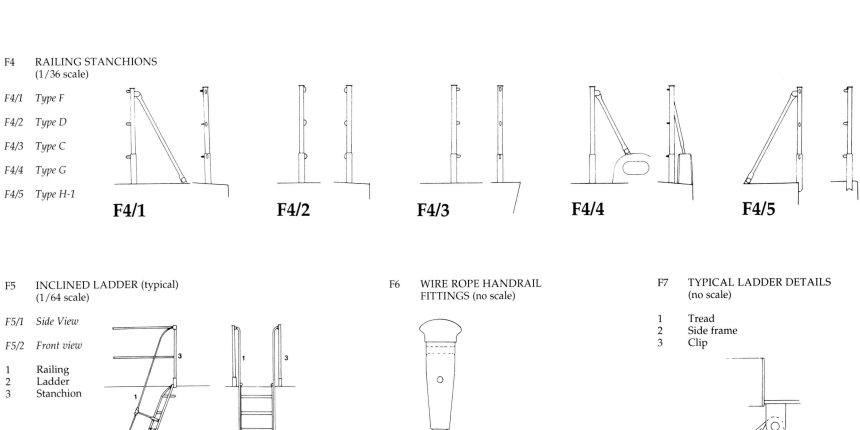

F4　RAILING STANCHIONS
(1/36 scale)

F4/1　*Type F*

F4/2　*Type D*

F4/3　*Type C*

F4/4　*Type G*

F4/5　*Type H-1*

F4/1　　**F4/2**　　**F4/3**　　**F4/4**　　**F4/5**

F5　INCLINED LADDER (typical)
(1/64 scale)

F5/1　*Side View*

F5/2　*Front view*

1　Railing
2　Ladder
3　Stanchion

F5/1　　**F5/2**

F6　WIRE ROPE HANDRAIL
FITTINGS (no scale)

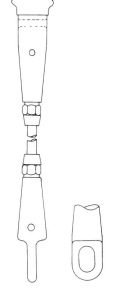

F6

F7　TYPICAL LADDER DETAILS
(no scale)

1　Tread
2　Side frame
3　Clip

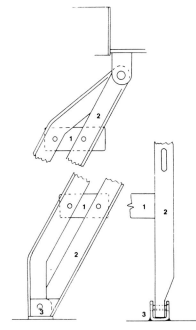

F7

F8　TYPICAL BENT STANCHION
(no scale)

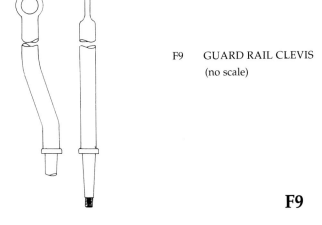

F8

F9　GUARD RAIL CLEVIS
(no scale)

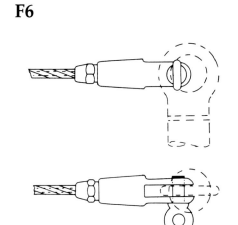

F9

F Fittings

F10 TYPICAL STRAIGHT STANCHION (1/12 scale)

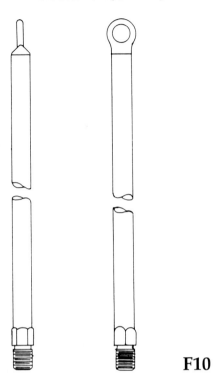

F10

F11 TYPICAL WIRE ROPE AND STANCHION AROUND DECK HATCH (1/48 scale)

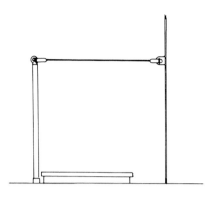

F11

F12 FIRE PLUG (1/24 scale)

1   Bracket
2   Nozzle
3   Hose
4   Wyegate
5   Self-cleaning strainer
6   Adjustable spanner
7   Fire plug

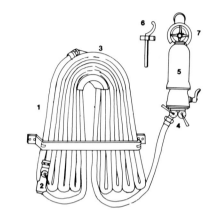

F12

F13 SELF-CLEANING STRAINER FOR FIRE NOZZLE (no scale)

1   2½in inlet
2   2½in outlet
3   Operating handle
4   Strainer
5   Flushing outlet

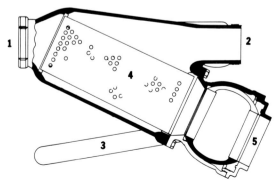

F13

F14 TYPE A REEL (1/16 scale)

F14/1 Side view

1   End plate
2   Lightening hole
3   Support bracket
4   Brake

F14/2 Front View

1   End plate
2   Support bracket
3   Reel drum
4   Axle
5   Wire rope

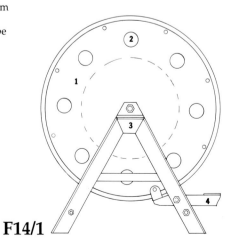

F14/1

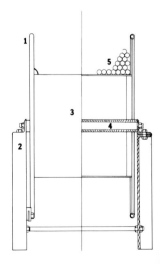

F14/2

F15   TYPE B REEL (1/12 scale)

F15/1 *Side view*

1   End plate
2   Lightening hole
3   Support bracket
4   Brake

F15/2 *Front View*

1   End plate
2   Support bracket
3   Reel drum
4   Axle
5   Separators

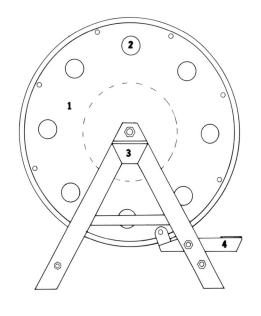

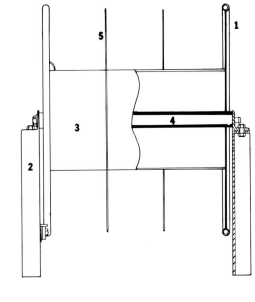

F15/1   **F15/2**

F16   DETACHABLE LINK (1/8 scale)

F16/1 *Assembled*

1   Lead ball
2   Tapered forelock pin
3   Lugged forelock
4   Link body

F16/2 *Disassembled*

1   Lead ball
2   Tapered forelock pin
3   Lugged forelock
4   Link body

F17   STOCKLESS ANCHOR (1/40 scale)

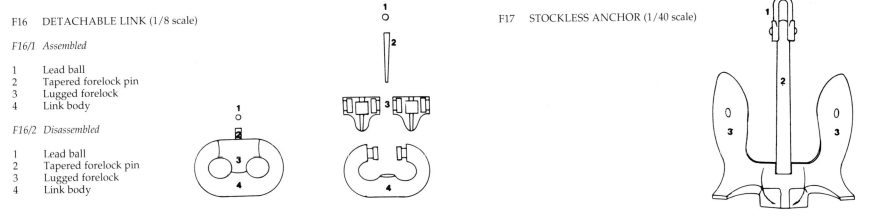

F16/1   **F16/2**   **F17**

F Fittings

F18   AIRCRAFT HANDLING/CARGO
        BOOM (1/24 scale)

F18/1 Boom end, side view

F18/2 Boom end, top view

F18/3 Boom end, end view

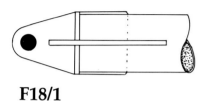

F18/1

F18/2

F18/3

F18/4 Boom clevis, side view

F18/5 Boom clevis, front view

F18/6 Boom clevis, top view

F18/7 Boom clevis, bottom view

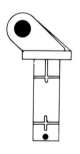

F18/6

F18/7

F18/4   **F18/5**

F18/8 Boom and clevis assembly

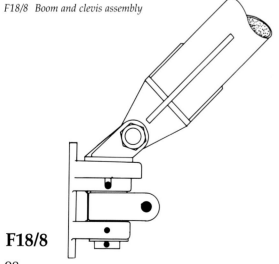

F18/8

98

F19   SINGLE ROLLER CHOCK
        (1/32 scale)

F19/1 Side view

F19/2 Top view

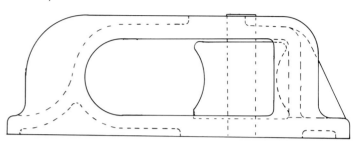

F19/1

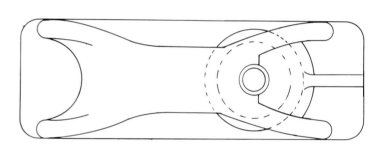

F19/2

F20   CLOSED CHOCK (1/48 scale)

F20/1 Side view

F20/2 Top view

F20/1

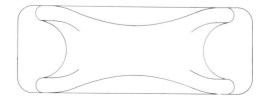

F20/2

F21   12in SIGNAL LAMP (1/12 scale)

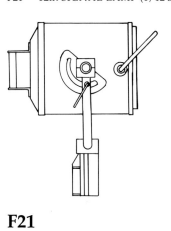

F22   24in SEARCHLIGHT (1/48 scale)

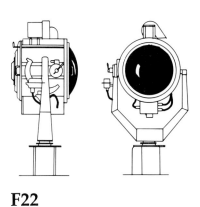

F23   PELORUS (1/32 scale)

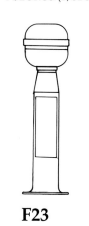

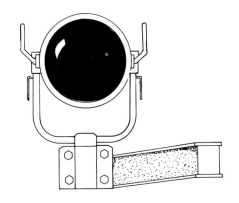

F21

F22

F23

F24   SKY LOOKOUT (1/40 scale)

F25   10in BITT (1/24 scale)

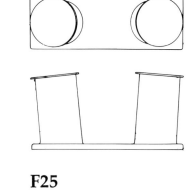

F25

F24

G Boats

G1   26ft MOTOR WHEELBOAT MK1
     (1/40 scale)

Gambier Bay carried two standard 26ft motor
whaleboats. There were a number of versions of
this type which were used interchangeably, two
of which are presented in this section.

G1/1   *Plan view, decked version*

G1/2   *Outboard profile, decked version,
        showing outline of canopy*

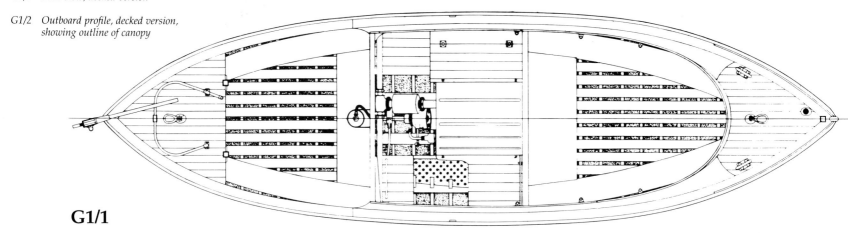

G1/1

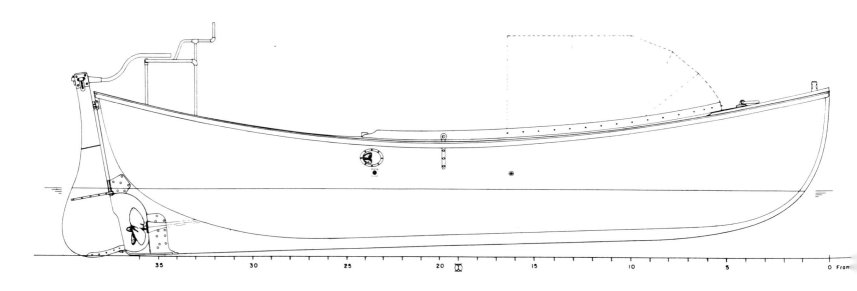

G1/2

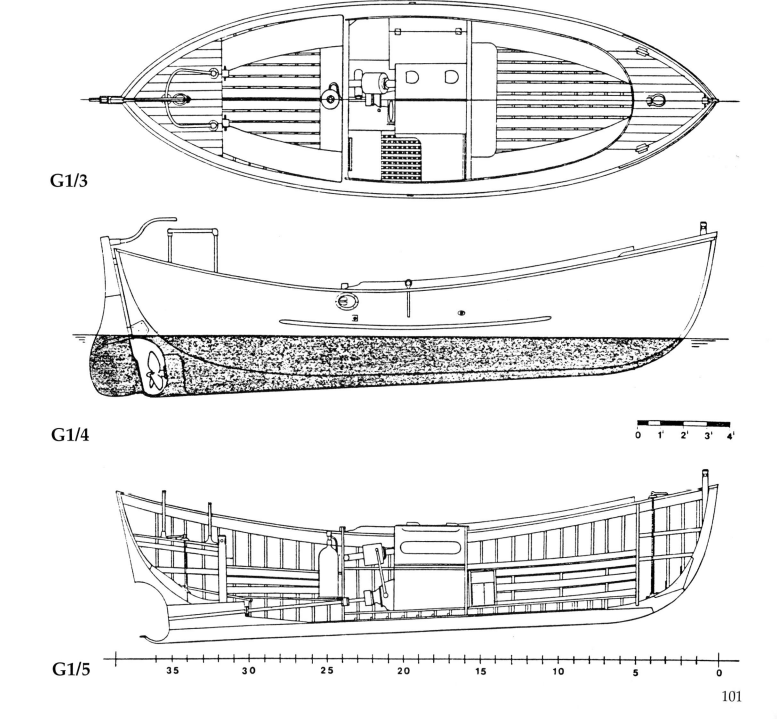

G1/3   *Plan view, undecked version (1/48 scale)*

G1/4   *Outboard profile, undecked version*
          (1/48 scale)

G1/5   *Inboard profile, undecked version*
          (1/48 scale)

G1/3

G1/4

0 1' 2' 3' 4'

G1/5   35   30   25   20   15   10   5   0

G Boats

G2   LINES AND SECTIONS, 26ft
       MOTOR WHALEBOAT
       (1/40 scale)

G2/1   *Plan view*

G2/2   *Elevation*

G2/3   *Stations*

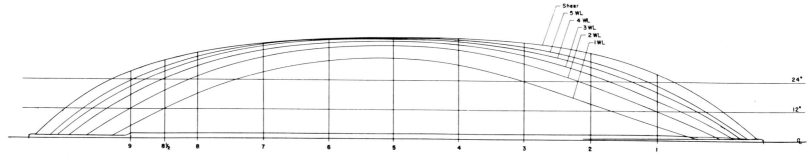

G2/1

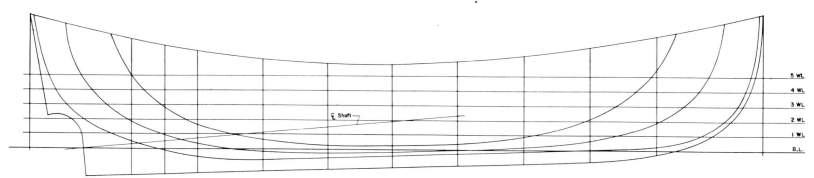

G2/2

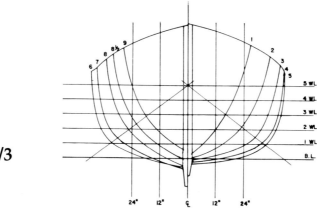

G2/3

G3 LONGITUDINAL SECTIONS, 26ft
MOTOR WHALEBOAT
(1/40 scale)

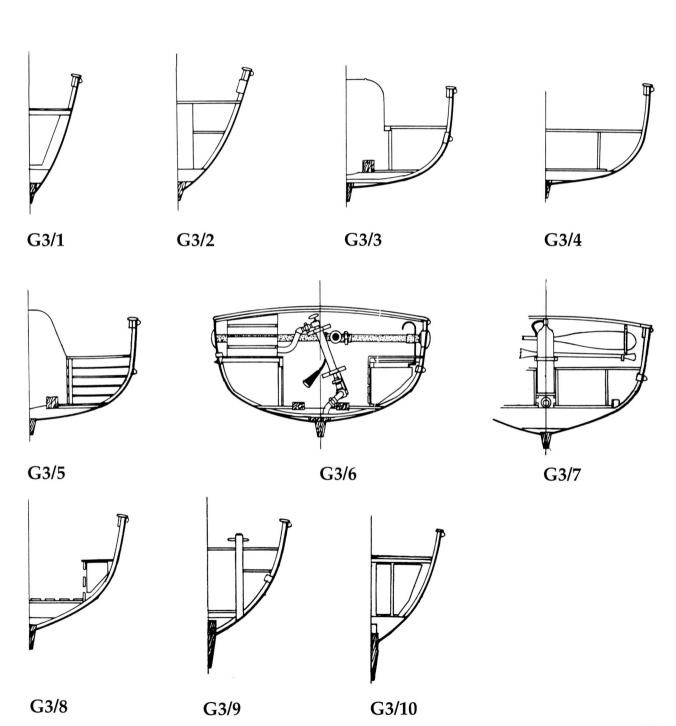

G3/1   **G3/2**   **G3/3**   **G3/4**

G3/5   **G3/6**   **G3/7**

G3/8   **G3/9**   **G3/10**

103

G Boats

G4 LIFTING ARRANGEMENT
(1/48 scale)

1   Double block
2   Raymond releasing block
3   Lifting eye
4   Lifting eye support

G5 RAYMOND RELEASING HOOK
(1/24 scale)

1   Block body
2   Sheave
3   Sheave pin
4   Main hook
5   Lifting eye
6   Safety hook

G6 25-MAN LIFERAFT (1/32 scale)

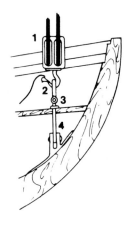

G4

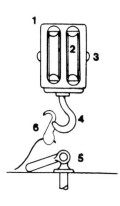

G5

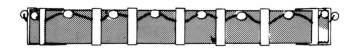

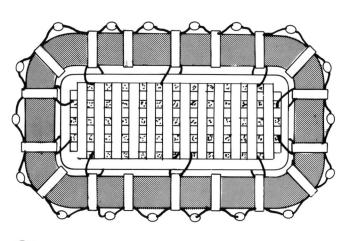

G6

G7 FLOATER NET (no scale)

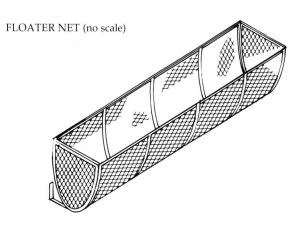

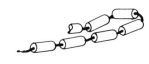

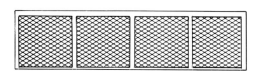

G7

H Flight deck arrangements

H1   ARRESTING GEAR
            ARRANGEMENT (1/28 scale)

1   Sheave
2   Cable
3   Turnbuckle
4   Cable support
5   Flight deck

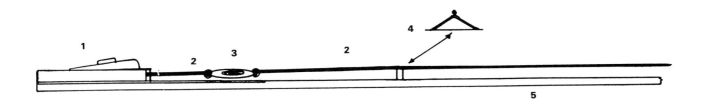

H1

H2   ARRESTOR WIRE SHEAVE AND
            PLATE (1/28 scale)

H2/1   Section through chafing plate

H2/1

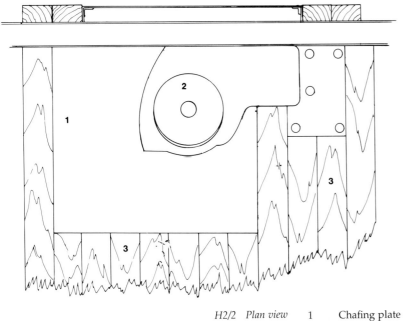

H2/2

H2/2   Plan view   1   Chafing plate
                            2   Sheave
                            3   Planking

H3   ARRESTOR WIRE SHEAVE AND
            BARRIER ARM (no scale)

1   Chafing plate
2   Turnbuckle
3   Sheave
4   Crash barrier arm
5   Flight deck lip
6   Flight deck planking
7   Barrier wires

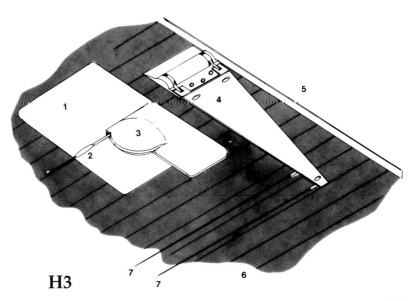

H3

H Flight deck arrangements

H4   AIRCRAFT TIEDOWN STRIP

H4/1   *Tiedowns and planking forward*
        (1/384 scale)

1   Tiedown
2   Catapult
3   Planking
4   Elevator
5   Expansion joint

H4/2   *Tiedown strip (1/2 scale)*

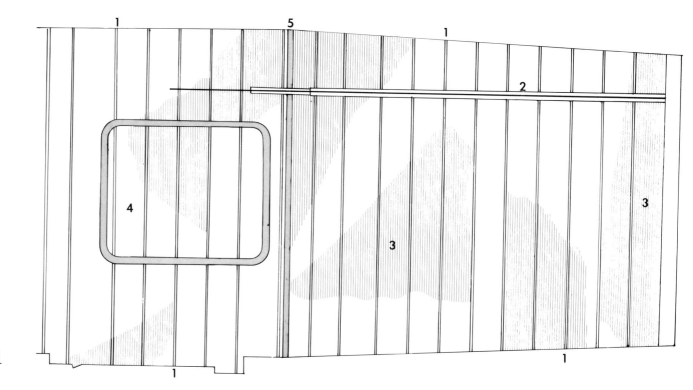

H4/1

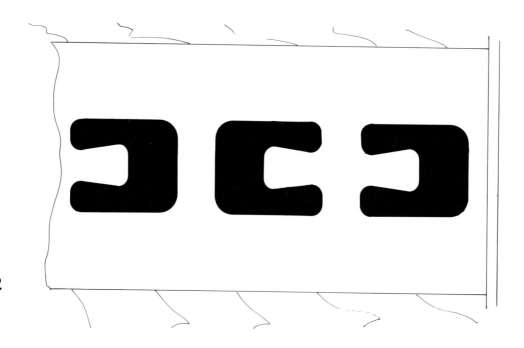

H4/2

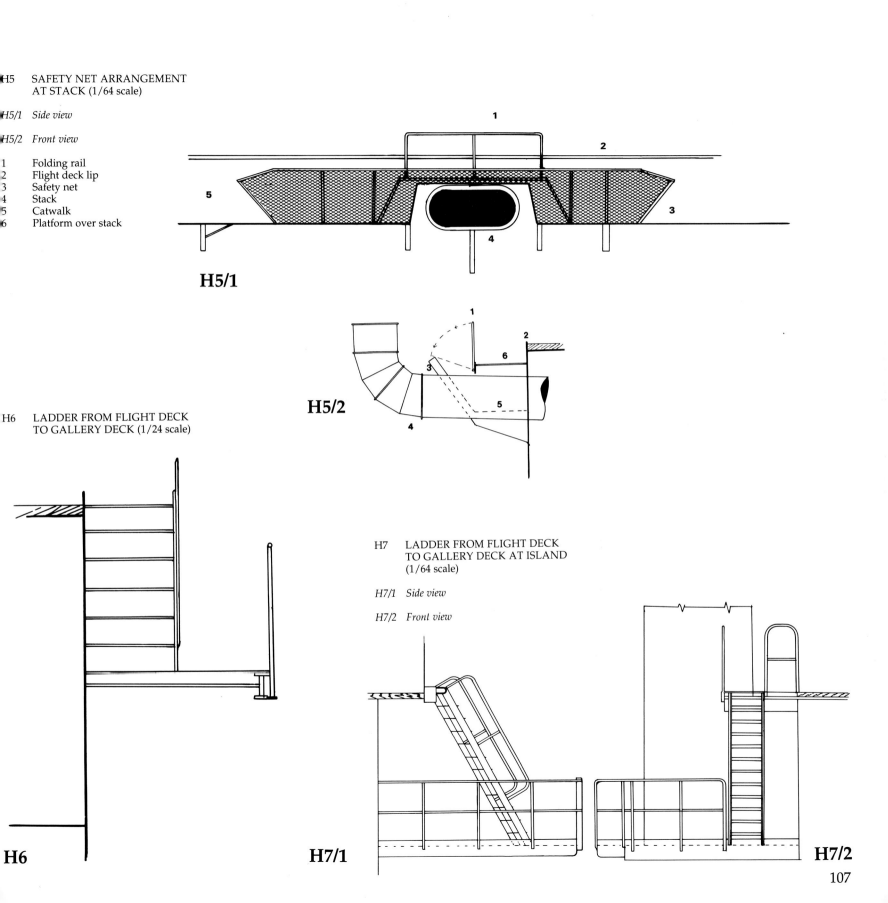

H5 SAFETY NET ARRANGEMENT
AT STACK (1/64 scale)

H5/1 *Side view*

H5/2 *Front view*

1 Folding rail
2 Flight deck lip
3 Safety net
4 Stack
5 Catwalk
6 Platform over stack

H5/1

H5/2

H6 LADDER FROM FLIGHT DECK
TO GALLERY DECK (1/24 scale)

H7 LADDER FROM FLIGHT DECK
TO GALLERY DECK AT ISLAND
(1/64 scale)

H7/1 *Side view*

H7/2 *Front view*

H6

H7/1

H7/2

I Aircraft

I1   FM-2 WILDCAT (1/96 scale)

I1/1   Front view

I1/2   Top view

I1/3   Side view

I1/4   Bottom view

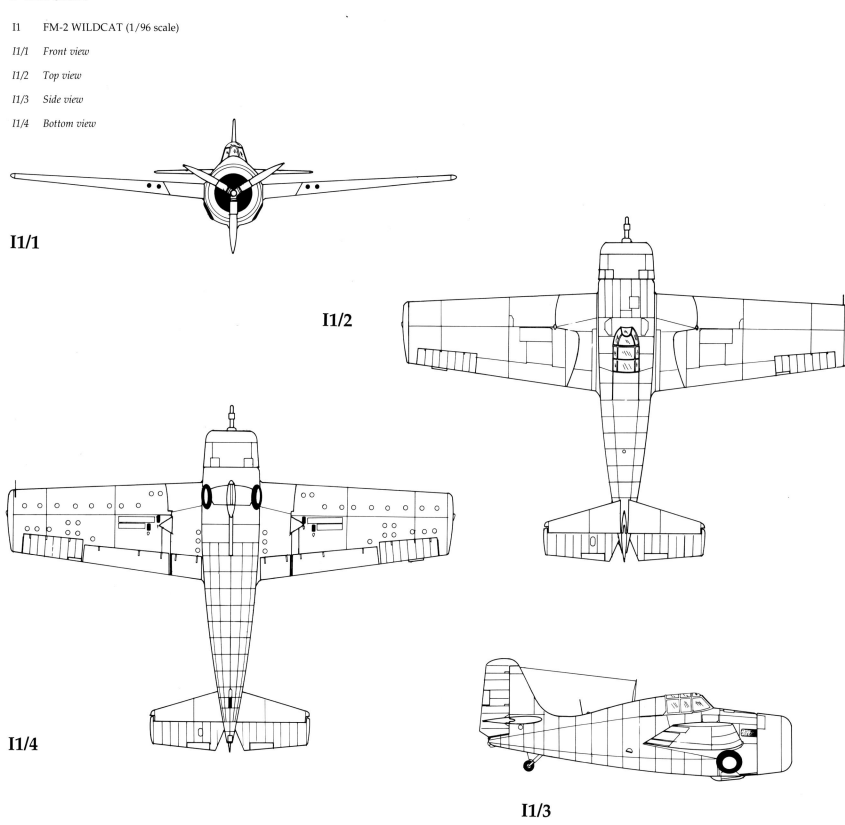

I1/1

I1/2

I1/4

I1/3

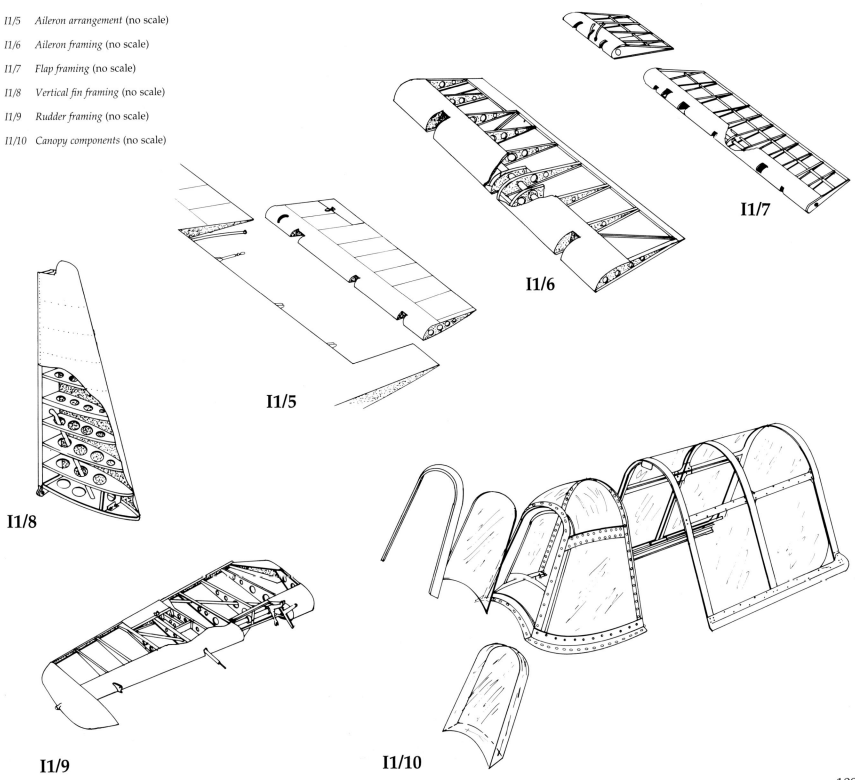

I1/5   *Aileron arrangement* (no scale)

I1/6   *Aileron framing* (no scale)

I1/7   *Flap framing* (no scale)

I1/8   *Vertical fin framing* (no scale)

I1/9   *Rudder framing* (no scale)

I1/10   *Canopy components* (no scale)

I1/7

I1/6

I1/5

I1/8

I1/9

I1/10

I Aircraft

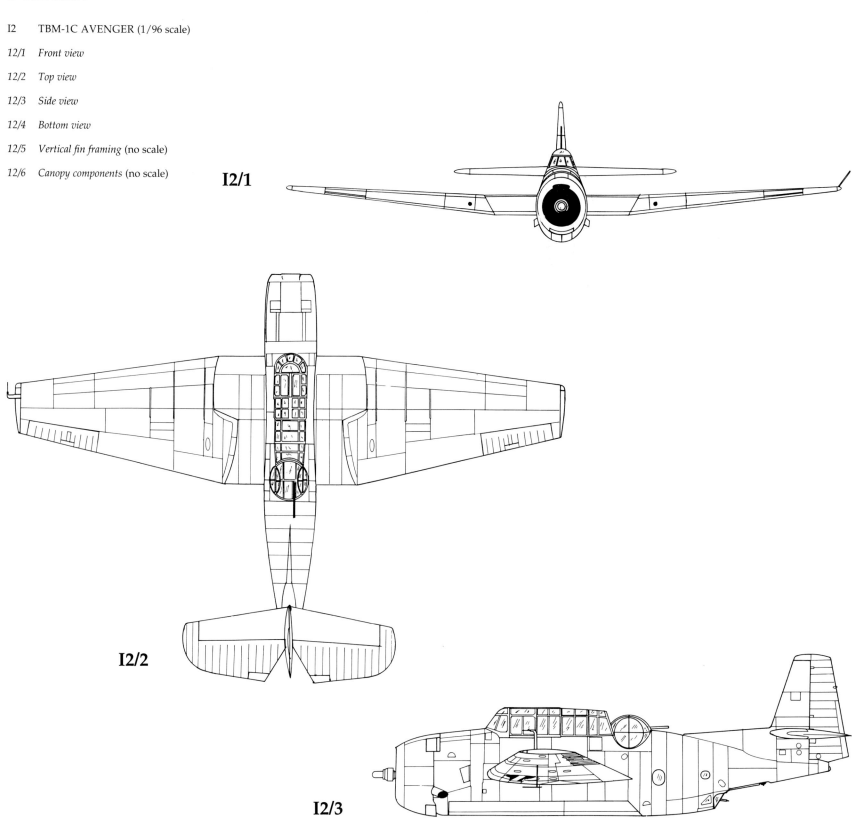

I2/1

I2/2

I2/3

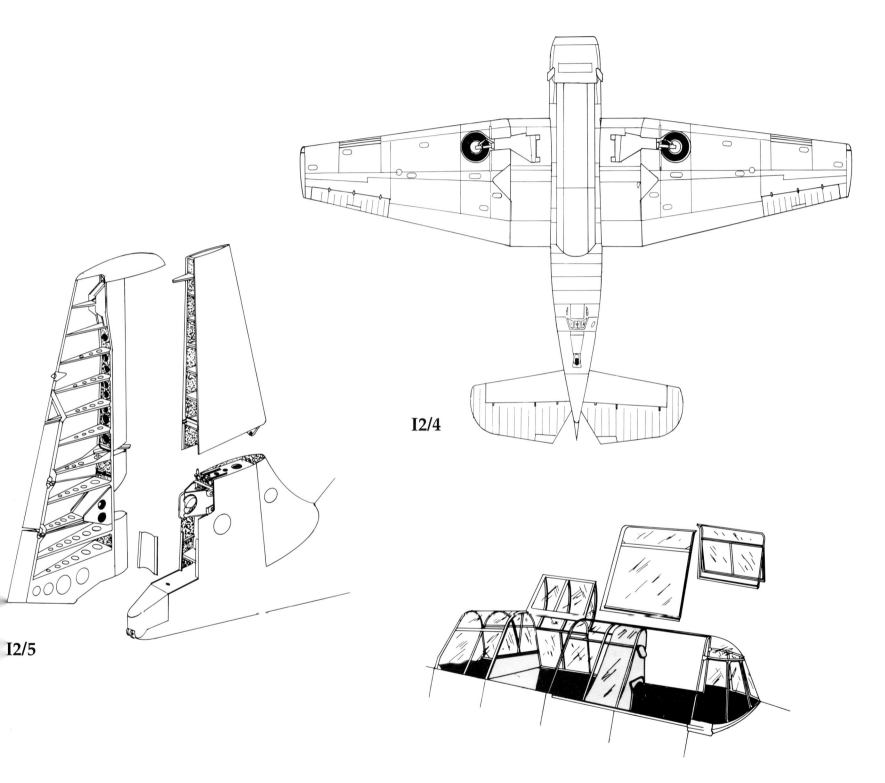

I2/4

I2/5

I2/6

J Camouflage

J   CAMOUFLAGE

J1/1   *Port side*

J1/2   *Starboard side*

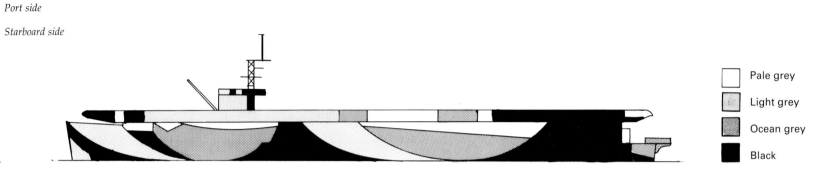

J1/1

Pale grey

Light grey

Ocean grey

Black

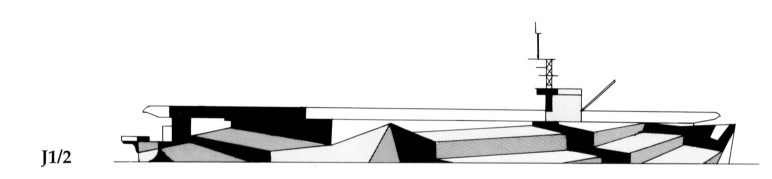

J1/2

K   BATTLE DAMAGE

Circles shown indicate known hits. Numbers
correspond to those in the text.

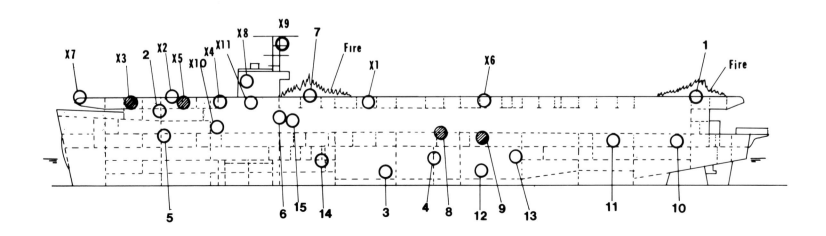